School Self Evaluation, Improvement and Inspection

a practical guide for school governors

Martin Pounce

Adamson Publishing

© Martin Pounce 2012

Published by Adamson Publishing Ltd
8 The Moorings, Norwich NR3 3AX
tel: 01603 623336 fax: 01603 624767
e-mail: info@adamsonbooks.com
www.adamsonbooks.com

ISBN 978-0-948543-38-8

British Library Cataloguing in Publication Data
A catalogue record for this book is available from the British Library

Cover design by Geoff Shirley

All rights reserved. Individual pages of this book may be photocopied for its own use by a governing body that has purchased the book. With this exception, no part of this publication may be reproduced, stored in a retrieval system, or be transmitted, in any form or by any means, electronic, mechanical, photocopying, recording or otherwise, without the prior permission of the publishers. Such permission, if granted, is subject to a fee depending on the nature of the use.

Printed and bound by Impress Print, Corby

Contents

1. Introduction   5
2. Evaluating your school's impact on pupil achievement   10
3. How effective is teaching?   22
4. Behaviour and safety   29
5. Leadership and management   35
6. Overall effectiveness: the quality of the education provided in the school   45
7. Turning self-evaluation into school improvement   49
8. Getting the most from Ofsted inspection   51

Appendixes   55
    A Inspection of faith schools
    B Inspection of boarding provision

Index   56

The author

Martin Pounce has spent 40 years working in education: as a teacher, teacher-centre leader and, since the mid 1990s, as an education officer in two local authorities. He has been closely involved in governor training and development since 1992 when he joined AGIT (Action for Governors' Information and Training) as Development Officer. Martin has been a governor in two secondary schools in Dudley and Coventry, in a Southwark primary school in the late 1990s and then at an infants school in Buckinghamshire. He is a governor at a special school and an additional governor in a primary school. He also chairs an Interim Executive Board.

Martin shares his time between work for Oxfordshire Governor Services and consultancy to support colleagues working with governors in other authorities. He can be contacted via email, martin.pounce@btinternet.com.

Acknowledgements

This book started out as a leaflet co-produced by Co-ordinators of Governor Services in the Eastern Region (ERCOGS) and builds on the thinking of many colleagues in the group. My wife, Susan, who is both an inspector and chair of an IEB, has provided many examples of good practice which have found their way into the book. My colleagues in Oxfordshire continuously develop my ideas, while questioning from the many governors I have worked with over the years as well as my own experience have helped me to think through the practicalities of governor involvement in school self-evaluation and improvement. Stephen Adamson's incisive editing has given this book clearer shape. Extracts from the Evaluation Schedule are reproduced by kind permission of Ofsted.

I acknowledge all these contributions while accepting full responsibility for any errors and omissions.

Martin Pounce
March 2012

Ofsted documents

This book refers frequently to Ofsted inspections. To see Ofsted's key documents – *The Evaluation Schedule for Schools*, *The Framework for School Inspection* and *Conducting School Inspections* – go to the Ofsted website, www.ofsted.gov.uk, and click on Forms and guidance > Schools.

Academies and maintained schools

Some official publications talk separately about "schools" and "academies". However, academies are schools too, so throughout this book the term "school" includes both.

1. Introduction

This book is designed to help governors (and headteachers) to get into the skin of an inspector and to make the sorts of judgements that inspectors make, so that:

- inspection will contain no surprises (and generate fewer fears!)
- your school doesn't have to wait for Ofsted to tell you what you need to do
- greater clarity about the school's strengths and weaknesses can translate into a clearer consensus about school improvement priorities
- the governing body can provide a more informative account of the school to all stakeholders
- most important of all, the school can provide a really good education for all its pupils.

Recent developments in inspection

Significant changes have been put in place from the previous inspection system, including:

- removal of the standard Self Evaluation Form and an expectation that schools will record the results in ways which best suit their particular circumstances
- a sharper focus on four areas by the which the effectiveness of schools is judged:
  - Pupil Achievement – see chapter 2
  - Teaching – see chapter 3
  - Behaviour and safety – see chapter 4
  - Leadership and management – see chapter 5

  and the inclusion of judgements about the breadth of young people's experience of education in the overall effectiveness judgement – see chapter 6

- increasingly explicit statements that "satisfactory" is not good enough, and the proposal that from September 2013 the grade 3 category will be redesignated as "requires improvement"
- the introduction of an on-line questionnaire for parents, Parent View – see chapter 8
- the proposed move to no-notice inspections becoming the standard procedure.

The governing body's role in self-evaluation

Schools are complicated places with a lot going on and heaps of data. School self-evaluation may therefore appear to be a highly technical process which should be left to the professionals. But while much of the detailed work will be undertaken by school staff, governing bodies would be abdicating their responsibility if they were to leave it entirely to the professionals.

The governing body is accountable to all the school's stakeholders and needs to know and understand for itself what the school is doing well and what it needs to improve. In taking its responsibilities seriously a governing body will help their headteacher to be reflective and analytical. With so much information available it can be difficult to see the wood for the trees.

When a senior leadership team knows it has to boil down all that it knows from its analysis of school data to produce an accurate summary for governors, it concentrates the mind and clarifies analysis. Finally, since self-evaluation is the proper foundation of all the strategic decisions governing bodies make to secure continuous development in schools, as a governor you cannot be strategic without the understanding that comes from proper involvement.

In May 2011 Ofsted published a very informative report, *School Governance: Learning from the best*, which listed key characteristics of outstanding governing bodies. The report found that in these:

- Positive relationships between governors and school leaders are based on trust, openness and transparency. Effective governing bodies systematically monitor their school's progress towards meeting agreed development targets. Information about what is going well and why, and what is not going well and why, is shared. Governors consistently ask for more information, explanation or clarification. This makes a strong contribution to robust planning for improvement.

- Governors are well informed and knowledgeable because they are given high-quality, accurate information that is concise and focused on pupil achievement. This information is made accessible by being presented in a wide variety of formats, including charts and graphs.

- Outstanding governance supports honest, insightful self-evaluation by the school, recognising problems and supporting the steps needed to address them.

- School leaders and governors behave with integrity and are mutually supportive. School leaders recognise that governors provide them with a different perspective which contributes to strengthening leadership. The questions they ask challenge assumptions and support effective decision-making.

Conversely, the 2011 annual report from the HM Chief Inspector noted that "inspection findings show that where governance is less effective a lack of transparency and accurate information restricts the ability of the governing body to monitor the work of the school systematically".

The central purpose of this book is to demonstrate both to headteachers and other governors that governor involvement in school self-evaluation is genuinely helpful to school leadership teams. As *Learning from the Best* demonstrates, outstanding governing bodies are already receiving clear and timely information, governors are using it effectively, asking questions where they need clarification, challenging assumptions and helping to identify priorities for improvement.

Focused self-evaluation

This book is not supposed to be a recipe for a nervous breakdown! In order to cover the full range of school life, it suggests many lines of enquiry and a long list of questions. You are advised not to try to answer – or ask – them all at once. There will be aspects described in the book where as a governing body you will be entirely satisfied that you already know enough. However, if you have not been much involved in school self-evaluation up to now, you may feel that there are lots of areas that you need to explore; but if you want to be strategic and avoid defensiveness you will agree a limited number of the most important aspects to start with and hold others back for later consideration.

It will be up to each individual governing body to agree with the headteacher which are the priority areas where the involvement of governors in seeking and examining evidence will make the biggest difference. These decisions will be informed by information that the headteacher has supplied over recent months. You will want to focus on aspects where you have little or no up-to-date information and those where recent information suggests weaknesses. There may need to be some collective plain speaking to ensure that uncomfortable areas are not brushed under the carpet. It is a key "critical friend" role of the governing body to address these areas before Ofsted inspection exposes them as evidence of inadequacies in leadership and management.

But how do you as a governing body get the overall picture and identify priorities? Each chapter contains suggestions of how self-evaluation information can be obtained, including: reports from the headteacher, other staff or outsiders; surveys of parents, pupils and staff; and governor visits.

Obtaining information for evaluation is made much easier with the cooperation of the headteacher, who is likely to be the main source of this essential information. In my earlier book *Headteachers and Governing Bodies* (Adamson Publishing, 2007), a whole chapter was devoted to the issue of reporting to the governing body.

Governors need an independent view of what "good" and "outstanding" look like in the different aspects of school life. Interspersed in the text are the latest (2012) Ofsted descriptors. Use these to check your perception of quality and impact in your own school. All descriptors are published on the Ofsted website at www.ofsted.gov.uk

When is evidence sufficient?

At times you may not be entirely satisfied with the evidence you are presented with by the headteacher or other member of the senior leadership team, and may feel you need to delve a little deeper to understand the true position. Sometimes considerably more scrutiny is justified; it demonstrates a governing body taking its responsibilities seriously and ensuring proper accountability. However, repeated questioning about every little detail will be irritating to headteachers and distract from important matters; most seriously it will demonstrate a complete lack of trust and undermine the partnership between head and governing body. You therefore need to judge which issues to make the focus of in-depth questioning. These will include matters of strategic significance such as

- pupil attainment and progress
- narrowing the gap
- behaviour and bullying.

They will also include aspects of school life where the consequences of things going wrong are potentially very serious, such as safeguarding procedures.

For all of these you should receive reports with explanations. You would be expected to seek clarification by asking questions. If the answers to those questions are clear and helpful and demonstrate openness on the part of the headteacher or relevant member of staff, that may be sufficient. If you judge that there may be more useful information and significant insights on this important aspect of school life and development you would be fully justified in asking further questions and quite possibly asking the headteacher to bring a more detailed report to another meeting. It may be appropriate for a governor to volunteer to work with the head on producing such a report.

If the governing body meets resistance it could be that:

- The questioning has strayed into operational matters or away from strategic issues – consider this possibility and if this is the case be prepared to withdraw.
- The headteacher resents the apparent lack of trust being exhibited – try to reach a shared understanding of why detailed questioning has been necessary in this case.

- The headteacher regards this as another in a long list of unrealistic demands imposed by the governing body – the governing body may need to reflect on the totality of its requests but the headteacher also needs to consider whether she or he understands and respects the role of governing bodies.
- The headteacher is not on top of this aspect or there is even something to hide – the governing body needs to ask itself whether there is something in their treatment of previous issues which has made the headteacher reluctant to be open with governors, and the headteacher needs to reflect on the advantages of sharing information with the governing body.

It should always be possible for a governing body to commission an external consultant to give a professional view in cases of significant doubt.

Update school self-evaluation regularly

Self-evaluation is much like painting the Forth Bridge. Over a period of three or five years so much about the school can change. The areas that the governing body originally identified as requiring development will have found their way on to the school's development plan and should have produced improvement. You may be hoping that some of the aspects you described as good have become outstanding. But equally, aspects that were previously good or outstanding could have slipped. An out-of-date self-evaluation statement is worse than useless.

There is a reluctance on the part of many perfectionist headteachers to complete a piece of self-evaluation. This is where an effective governing body comes into its own. By breaking down self-evaluation into its different aspects and then scheduling when each will be addressed, the governing body should be able to galvanise the necessary action and be able to "bank" each judgement before moving on to the next. It is not only too late to start self-evaluation but too late to finish it when the phone call from the inspector is received.

Getting incisive judgements in school self-evaluation

School self-evaluation should give a clear picture of how well the school is doing, provide proof of how you know what you know and show what you are doing to build on successes and remedy weaknesses.

It is important to base your judgements on Ofsted's descriptors in the Evaluation Schedule. Although Ofsted does not require the school to grade itself in each area, you should try to see which descriptor applies to you. Each of the chapters in this book that deal with an aspect of inspection starts with a "below the bottom line" box showing what inspectors would judge to be inadequate. If you can't confidently state that none of these statements apply, you will need to take urgent action to address the problem. Further into each chapter are the descriptors for "outstanding" and "good". You should use these to consider the evidence the school has collected and the judgement the head or senior leadership team has made. If you think the school is somewhere on the boundary you may agree a statement with the headteacher that identifies the things that the school will be doing in order to be securely in the higher grade. Descriptors for "satisfactory" are not included because every school should be aspiring to good or outstanding.

Ask:

- Does our evidence really justify the grade we are thinking of awarding ourselves? Your headteacher may be too modest or cautious, or over-generous.
- Do we have sufficient evidence to say confidently that our practice in this particular area is

consistent and effective?

- Does the list of development priorities represent our collective view? And if they are not already in our school improvement plan, what steps do we need to take?

Checking/making a judgement

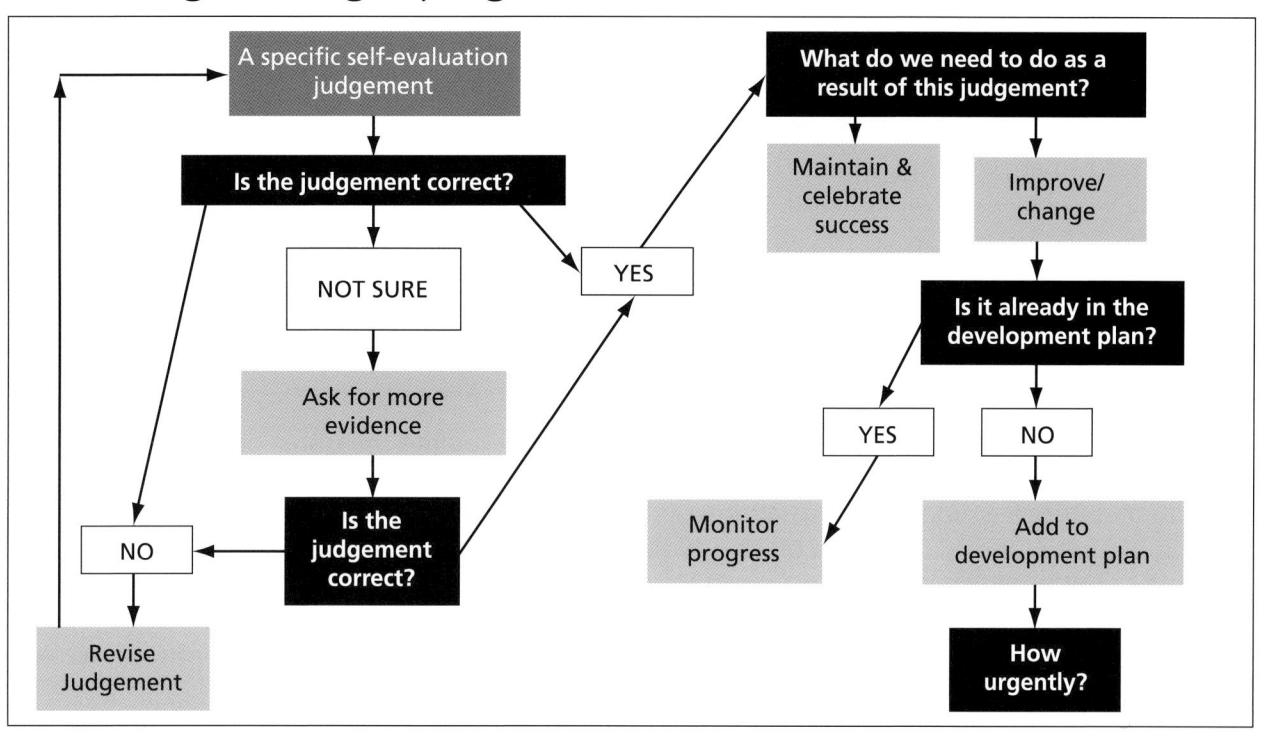

```
A specific self-evaluation judgement
        ↓
Is the judgement correct?
   ↓         ↓        ↘
NOT SURE    YES        What do we need to do as a result of this judgement?
   ↓                    ↓              ↓
Ask for more          Maintain &     Improve/
evidence              celebrate      change
   ↓                  success           ↓
Is the judgement                    Is it already in the
correct?                            development plan?
   ↓                                   ↓         ↓
NO → Revise Judgement                YES        NO
                                      ↓          ↓
                                  Monitor    Add to
                                  progress   development plan
                                                 ↓
                                             How urgently?
```

Checking a judgement

The above chart shows how governors might respond to a judgement proposed by the senior leadership team. For example, the judgement may be that the school is good in a particular area. But you may consider that you meet all the criteria in the Ofsted descriptor of "good" except for one. You may know that the school doesn't do it well enough and therefore you can only judge it satisfactory, or you may simply not have the evidence that the school does it to a good standard. If so you would ask the leadership team to show further evidence for the judgement.

The link between school self-evaluation and improvement

The purpose of school self-evaluation is to identify ways in which the school can be improved. If Ofsted's understanding of the features which make effective schools is at all accurate, using the evaluation framework to provide a focus, identifying the most important aspects where the school does not perform as well and prioritising action to address them will give the school the best chance of improving. Chapter 7 will briefly describe how governor involvement in school self-evaluation translates into effective school improvement planning.

Recording your improvement plans
A planning grid on page 50 allows you to record the judgements for your school in each Ofsted area together with your improvement priorities and the focus for further evaluation.

2 Evaluating your school's impact on pupil achievement

Evaluating the effect that your school has on the learning and progress of every pupil must be a key task for every governing body. Knowing the overall pattern of progress is not sufficient; schools need to analyse the progress of all groups, including those with special educational needs and those who have to overcome other barriers to learning if they are to succeed.

The long tail of under-achievement in the English education system compared with most OECD countries means that there is a huge challenge for all schools to "narrow the gap"– specifically that lower achieving pupils must be helped to progress at a faster rate to catch up. This does not imply that higher achievers should be asked to mark time; governors can also expect that the learning needs of the more able pupils are also met through extra challenge.

While progress measures will be relative to starting points, absolute measures of attainment are also important because they get pupils onto the next step in their schooling. The ability to read is a key to all future learning, and evaluating your school's success in teaching and promoting reading at ages 6 and 11 has been given a high national priority. Governors should worry most about the young people in mainstream schools who end Key Stage 4 with few or no qualifications and who are likely to be most vulnerable and marginalised in the years to come. That is not just a concern for secondary schools; the seeds of disillusionment with education may have been sown in primary school.

Although National Curriculum test and exam results are not the only measure of success, they provide a rich source of information to compare yourselves with similar schools. The online report

> **Below the bottom line – Ofsted's description of inadequate**
> Achievement is likely to be inadequate if any of the following apply:
>
> - Pupils' learning and progress overall, or the learning and progress of particular groups, is consistently below those of all pupils nationally given their starting point.
>
> - Learning and progress in any key subject or key stage, including the sixth form, lead to underachievement
>
> - The learning, quality of work and progress of disabled pupils and those who have special educational needs show that this group is underachieving.
>
> - Pupils' communication skills, including in reading and writing and proficiency in mathematics overall, or those of particular groups, are not sufficient for the next stage of education or training.
>
> - Attainment is consistently low showing little, fragile or inconsistent improvement , or is in decline.
>
> - There are wide gaps in attainment and in learning and progress between different groups of pupils and of all pupils nationally that are showing little sign of closing or are widening.
>
> - There are wide gaps in attainment and in learning and progress between different groups of pupils that are barely closing or are widening.

that is provided for each school analyses these results in many ways, producing a large volume of data. You can expect your headteacher and other senior staff to grapple on your behalf with all this and present the key points; but that does not relieve governors of the responsibility to understand what it shows.

This chapter will describe the sort of information that governors can expect their headteachers to share with them to evaluate pupils' learning, progress and attainment. This includes:

- pupil tracking, which gives teachers and heads a term-by-term understanding of the progress and attainment of every year group or class (pages 14–16)
- Fischer Family Trust data, which used in many schools as a basis for discussing challenging targets with teachers sand pupils (pages 16–18)
- monitoring of work in pupils' books by school leaders, which should show what pupils have learned and the progress they are making.
- the views of pupils, parents and carers on pupil progress.

RAISEonline

Every primary and secondary school receives an analysis of its data from the government in the form of RAISEonline (Reporting and Analysis for Improvement through School Self-Evaluation). This is a hefty document sent to schools electronically – usually in October – showing how your pupils' attainment and progress compares with previous years, with all schools nationally and with similar schools. But there are other sources of data that you can expect to use.

Individual governors can have access to their school's RAISEonline data on the internet with a password provided by the school's RAISEonline administrator. You will not be able to see the names of individual children – that level is confined to staff – but it does mean that you can see the full range of analysis about your school.

But beware: while it may be tempting and appear helpful for interested governors to do the analysis for the school, it is vital that school leadership has the skills and makes the time to undertake their own professional analysis of the data and to report the key points of that analysis to the governing body. If your senior leadership does not seem to have the skill to do this properly, you should ensure they are trained; if it does not have sufficient time, you should ask for a re-alignment of priorities.

If you are worried about the quality of analysis you receive you should seek advice from an external adviser, whether from the local authority, another headteacher with particular expertise or an external consultant.

Basic characteristics of the school

You will regularly hear statements such as "we have a high percentage of pupils entitled to Free School Meals (FSM) ..." or "we have a lot of social deprivation ..." The very first table in RAISEonline (overleaf) shows how your school compares with all other schools in the country. This is a very visual presentation to support – or moderate – these assertions.

Pupil progress

Progress can be measured from the time pupils join the school to the end of Key Stage 2, 4 or sixth form. Sometimes a single year's analysis will give a different picture from previous years; it could be a "blip" – up or down – or it could represent the beginning of a significant change. You should consider evidence from previous years to identify trends.

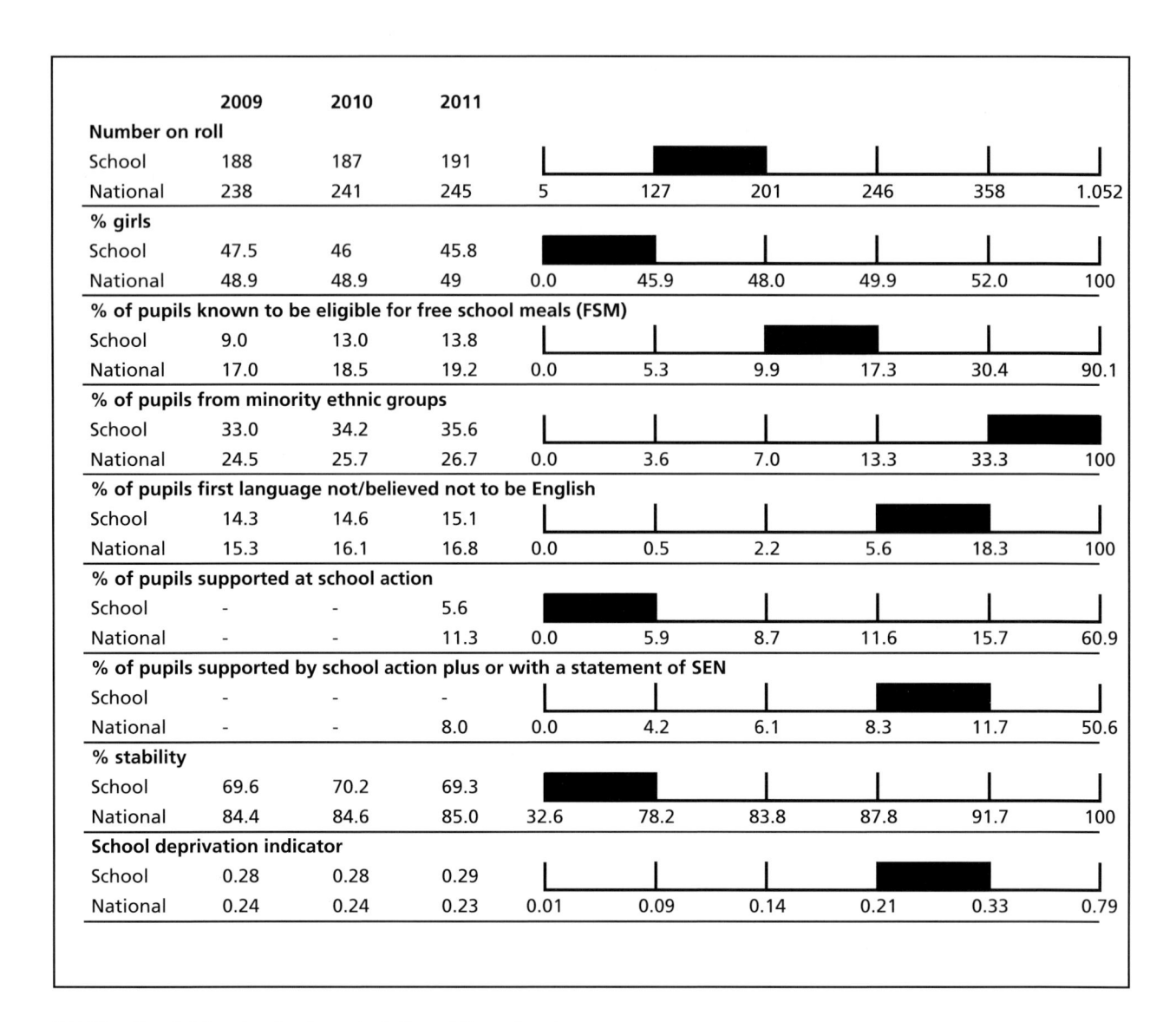

	2009	2010	2011					
Number on roll								
School	188	187	191					
National	238	241	245	5	127	201	246	358	1.052
% girls								
School	47.5	46	45.8					
National	48.9	48.9	49	0.0	45.9	48.0	49.9	52.0	100
% of pupils known to be eligible for free school meals (FSM)								
School	9.0	13.0	13.8					
National	17.0	18.5	19.2	0.0	5.3	9.9	17.3	30.4	90.1
% of pupils from minority ethnic groups								
School	33.0	34.2	35.6					
National	24.5	25.7	26.7	0.0	3.6	7.0	13.3	33.3	100
% of pupils first language not/believed not to be English								
School	14.3	14.6	15.1					
National	15.3	16.1	16.8	0.0	0.5	2.2	5.6	18.3	100
% of pupils supported at school action								
School	-	-	5.6					
National	-	-	11.3	0.0	5.9	8.7	11.6	15.7	60.9
% of pupils supported by school action plus or with a statement of SEN								
School	-	-	-					
National	-	-	8.0	0.0	4.2	6.1	8.3	11.7	50.6
% stability								
School	69.6	70.2	69.3					
National	84.4	84.6	85.0	32.6	78.2	83.8	87.8	91.7	100
School deprivation indicator								
School	0.28	0.28	0.29					
National	0.24	0.24	0.23	0.01	0.09	0.14	0.21	0.33	0.79

RAISEonline table – basic characteristics of the school

For primary schools the measure which is most readily available relates to progress during the four years of Key Stage 2 using attainment levels at the end of Key Stage 1 as the baseline. Schools also get the Early Years Foundation Stage Profile, which shows how children were assessed soon after they entered the school. For secondary schools the measure can be from the end of Key Stage 2 when most young people arrive at secondary school to the end of Key Stage 4.

The progress that pupils make above or below the average is called the "value added". Every year this is calculated as a statistical measure; at the end of Key Stage 2 the national average is 100 and for secondary schools 1,000. Most primary schools will score in the range of 99-101. Exceptionally, a small minority will have a value added score of 104 or 96.

How significant is this value added score? The answer is that it depends on the size of the cohort. RAISEonline contains a graph showing the distribution of all schools nationally with a mark to show where your school sits both in terms of value added – the vertical line – and in relative attainment – the horizontal line. The diagram overleaf shows a secondary example where value added rises from 940 to 1060. The median point on the vertical is 1000. (The range in the equivalent primary graph is 74–124 with the median at 100.) Relative attainment is plotted on the horizontal line; zero represents the median and the range is minus 60 to plus 60. (The range

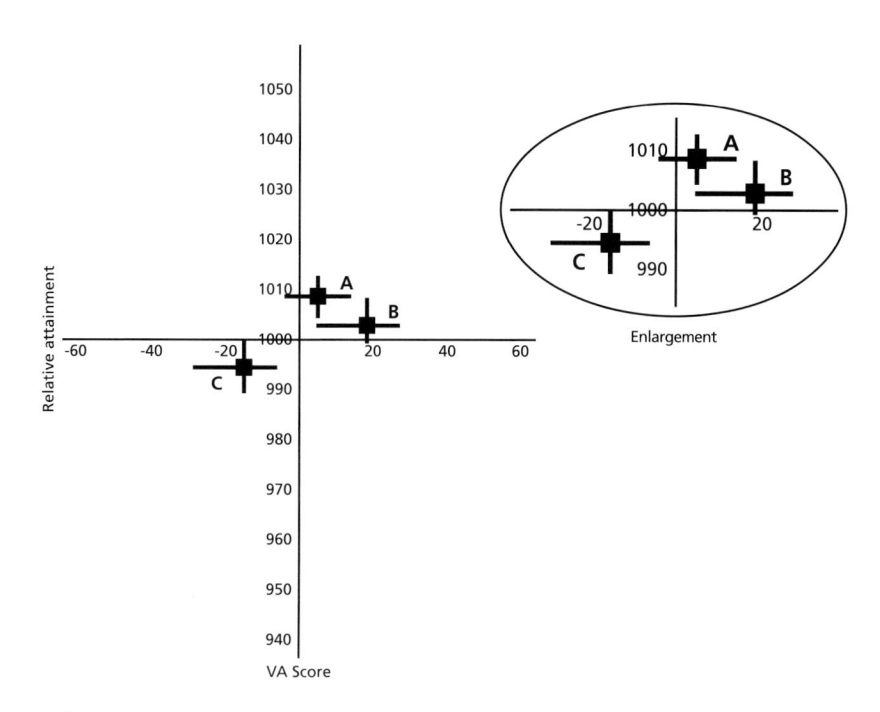

RAISEonline table – value added with "whiskers"

in the equivalent primary graph is minus 14 to plus 14.) The illustration shows the performance in three subject areas: English, humanities and mathematics. Each of these is shown by a square mark. This mark has "whiskers" above, below and to the sides. If a whisker crosses either of the median lines, the school is deemed to be "in line" with schools nationally. A school with a small cohort will have long "whiskers" and one of them is quite likely to cross the line; in that case whether your mark is well above or well below the horizontal line or a long way to the left or right of the vertical line, it is not statistically significant and the school is deemed to be in-line.

A represents English; pupil attainment and pupil progress both appear to be above average because the mark sits above the horizontal line and to the right of the vertical. However, the horizontal whisker crosses the vertical line and therefore pupil attainment is average. The vertical whisker does not cross the horizontal line which means that value added is above average. **B** represents maths. In this case attainment is above average but the vertical whisker crosses the horizontal line so progress is average. Governors in this school might be most concerned with humanities (**C**) where attainment is clearly below average but the vertical whisker touches the horizontal line so progress is actually average. In most schools these three subjects are likely to be grouped more closely; this notional school has a large variation between subjects for the purpose of illustration.

Tables develop this graph by highlighting significant figures, in blue for "sig-" and green for 'sig+". When you look at those tables you will hope to see lots of green. This will indicate progress significantly above average. If there are many blue boxes this indicates progress significantly below average; if you know that progress was even lower in previous years it may reveal the start of improvement. If there are no blue or green boxes progress will be broadly average.

The progress measure is the cause of one of the most common tensions between separate infant and junior school headteachers, arising from the fact that Key Stage 1 assessments are not made by outsiders but by the teachers. Infant heads naturally want their pupils to be assessed as high as possible at the end of key stage 1. However, if those pupil scores are inflated it creates a serious problem for the receiving junior school to demonstrate even average progress.

Secondary schools' RAISEonline data may reveal differences between subjects. School leaders may be able to explain that some of those differences are due to factors such as different calibre of pupils in option groups or staff illness, but it may also be a reflection of teaching quality that the senior leadership is already addressing. Certainly governors need to know about these issues, although you will need to be careful to avoid operational discussions or getting in the way of capability procedures.

Progress made by individual pupils and groups

The value added figure in the graph on page 13 lumps all the children in that cohort together and does not reveal the progress made by individual pupils. However, scatter graphs in RAISEonline provide valuable information about variations in individual pupil progress (without identifying individual children). These graphs plot the attainment of each child against the progress they might be expected to make based on the progress of similar pupils in other schools. The children represented by dots, squares or other symbols furthest from the diagonal line will have made the most progress if they are above the diagonal or the slowest progress if they are below.

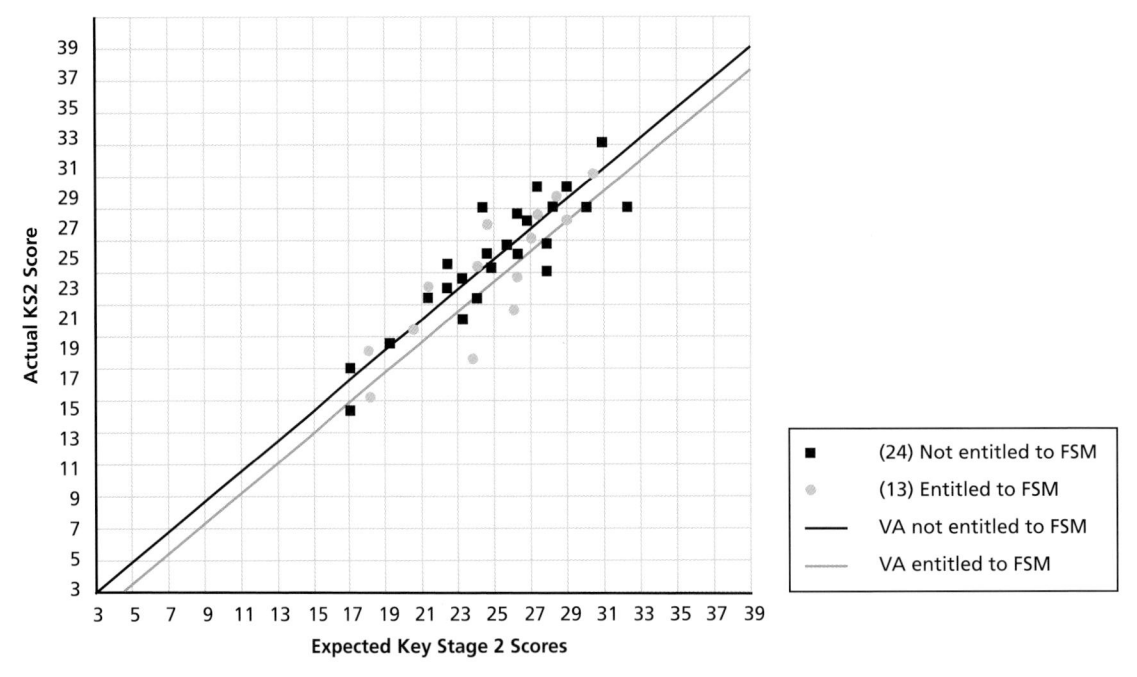

RAISEonline scatter graph (the original is in colour)

Scatter graphs can provide a visual indication of the school's success in narrowing the gap for particular groups of children. In the graph above pupils are distinguished by whether or not they are entitled to free school meals (FSM). Since April 2011 schools have been allocated the Pupil Premium (£600 per pupil in April 2012) to enable them to provide specific support for children and young people from disadvantaged families. You should analyse the impact of your spending of this extra money, and the scatter graph will be one source of data.

Other scatter graphs may reveal significant differences between boys and girls, children at various stages on the SEN register and those without SEN, different ethnic groups and pupils with English as an additional language. Discussion of these graphs may help governors to understand issues that need to be addressed or may indicate there has been a narrowing of gaps as the result of a strategy implemented previously.

> **Ofsted's description of outstanding pupil achievement**
> Almost all pupils, including where applicable disabled pupils and those with special educational needs, are making rapid and sustained progress in most subjects over time given their starting points. They learn exceptionally well and as a result acquire knowledge quickly and in depth and are developing their understanding rapidly in a wide range of different subjects across the curriculum, including those in the sixth form and areas of learning in the Early Years Foundation Stage. They develop and apply a wide range of skills to great effect, including reading, writing, communication and mathematical skills across the curriculum that will ensure they are exceptionally well prepared for the next stage in their education, training or employment. The standards of attainment of almost all groups of pupils are likely to be at least in line with national averages for all pupils with many above average. In exceptional circumstances where standards of attainment, including attainment in reading in primary schools, of any group of pupils are below those of all pupils nationally, the gap is closing dramatically over a period of time as shown by a wide range of attainment indicators.

Governors could ask: "where is the looked-after child (a child in the care of a local authority) on this graph?" All governing bodies have a responsibility to ensure that the school does all it can to overcome the disadvantages that being in the care system carries with it. Governors should be alert to the evidence of the impact of their policies and school practice on this vulnerable group.

Tracking pupil progress in all year groups

RAISEonline only provides data for the end of key stages but you need to know how much the school understands about the progress pupils are making in the intervening years. There is a variety of software tools that teachers can use to track individual progress, and your school will almost certainly be using one of them.

The national expectation is that children in primary and secondary schools will make one full level of progress every two years between the end of key stage 1 and the end of key stage 4. Primary teachers are now expert in dividing levels into three sub-levels. A child who has only just progressed from Level 1 into Level 2 will be said to be at level 2c; a child who is securely in level 2 will be deemed to be at level 2b; while a child who is not quite at level 3 will be judged a level 2a.

The national expectation therefore is that a child who is judged a secure level 2b at age 7 will achieve at least level 4b by age 11. That would only constitute "satisfactory" progress. The child will have progressed six sub-levels in the four years of key stage 2. This means that if the expectation is to be fulfilled, the school must aim that every child makes two sub-levels of progress each year. If a child does make two sub-levels each year he or she will have exceeded the expectation – progressing, say from 2b to 5c – and that will be deemed good progress. (If every child made two sub-levels progress every year in primary and secondary school they would be succeeding at GCSE in Year 9!). But a school where children make only one sub-level of progress each year would be falling very badly behind (a 2b child at age 7 would only get to 3a by age 11).

With the aid of their tracking software, teachers can identify the children who are not making at least satisfactory progress and quickly put in place suitable interventions.

You can ask to see progress summary sheets. They show at a glance which year groups are doing well and the areas where the school should be concentrating support. The illustrations overleaf are part of a summary sheet that also shows Writing and Numeracy attainment and progress. This uses a traffic light system to indicate where progress is above average, average, or below average. In this monochrome version the dark shading represents red for "below" attainment

Reading Attainment
% attaining or exceeding nationally expected level

Year (& cohort)	Autumn 2011 below	Autumn 2011 ave.	Autumn 2011 above	Spring 2012 below	Spring 2012 ave.	Spring 2012 above	Summer 2012 below	Summer 2012 ave.	Summer 2012 above
Y1 (30)	**33**	46	15						
Y2 (29)	20	41	*38*						
Y3 (25)	24	56	20						
Y4 (20)	15	45	*40*						
Y5 (30)	**30**	43	18						
Y6 (30)	**42**	28	30						

Reading Progress
% making or exceeding nationally expected progress

Year (& cohort)	Autumn 2011 I	Autumn 2011 S	Autumn 2011 G	Spring 2012 I	Spring 2012 S	Spring 2012 G	Summer 2012 I	Summer 2012 S	Summer 2012 G
Y1 (30)	12	81	7						
Y2 (29)	9	69	*22*						
Y3 (25)	16	80	4						
Y4 (20)	5	70	*25*						
Y5 (30)	**21**	71	6						
Y6 (30)	6	76	18						
SEN	6	67	*27*						
FSM	8	65	*27*						
Boys	12	66	22						

Key
I   Inadequate
S   Satisfactory
G   Good

Progress summary sheets

and "inadequate" progress. The medium shading represents green for "above" attainment and "good" progress. The unshaded sections would be coloured amber to highlight "in line" attainment and "average" progress.

Management can run into difficulties in tracking progress when teacher assessment is inconsistent. It is important therefore to ensure that the "levelling" of children's work is carried out collaboratively with other colleagues in the school and with staff from other schools. You should check that this is secure – otherwise the information you receive may turn out to be meaningless.

Fischer Family Trust data

RAISEonline is not the only source of information that schools use to judge their impact on pupils' learning. Many schools use Fischer Family Trust (FFT) data to help staff set targets for individual pupils and for a year cohort.

The Fischer Family Trust was founded by Mike Fischer CBE, co-founder of RM plc (Research Machines), to improve the use of data in UK education systems. The key feature of FFT analysis is the progress that pupils make from one key stage to the next and a comparison of individual pupils with similar pupils in similar schools. FFT receives data from the government including the results of every pupil in England and Wales. This enables it to establish norms for pupil progress, for example that:

- Pupils who average level 2b at KS1 are most likely to achieve level 4b at KS2
- Half of the pupils who averaged level 4 at KS2 are likely to gain 5 or more good GCSE grades.

Evaluating your school's impact on pupil achievement

FFT provides schools with estimates of the percentage of pupils that might attain particular standards. It offers four different estimates:

A – based on progress made last year by pupils nationally with similar prior attainment, gender and month of birth

B – based on the Type A estimate adjusted for a range of school context indicators

D – based on the Type B estimate adjusted to be consistent with the performance last year of schools at the 25th percentile in terms of value added.

A fourth estimate– the figures in boxes – is based on the school's value-added performance over the past three years.

———— Estimate Range ————

Academic Year 2011/12 — *24 pupils*

English and Maths Level 4+	[71%] 76% (B)	76% (A)	82% (D)
English and Maths Level 5+	[21%] 27% (A)	35% (B)	35% (D)
English Level 4+	[78%] 80% (B)	80% (A)	85% (D)
English Level 5+	[29%] 34% (A)	34% (B)	42% (D)
English 2 Levels progress	[81%] 87%	87% (B)	92% (D)
Mathematics Level 4+	83% (B) [84%]	84% (A)	88% (D)
Mathematics Level 5+	[35%] 42% (A)	42% (B)	50% (D)
English 2 levels progress	84% (B) [84%]	84% (A)	90% (D)
Science Level 4+	86% (B)	86% (A) [88%]	91% (D)
Science Level 5+	42% (A)	42% (B)	52% (D) [60%]

Fischer Family Trust estimates for a sample primary school (extract)

For secondary schools, the end of Key Stage 4 estimates table (not shown) take account prior attainment at both Year 6 and Year 9. Estimates include:

- 5+ A*-C passes
- 5+ A*-C passes including English and mathematics
- 5+ A*-G passes
- 5+ A*-G passes including English and mathematics
- Points Score Capped
- English three levels progress
- Mathematics three levels progress.

In all cases estimates are given from Year 6 and Year 9 starting points. The final two rows show percentages of pupils estimated to make two Levels of progress from Year 9 to Year 11.

FFT also provides a list of individual pupils showing their chances of gaining particular standards at the end of Key Stage 2 or Key Stage 4 based upon their prior attainment and other factors listed above. Teachers should use these to challenge and support their students to do as well as they can – "FFT shows that you have a 20 percent chance of achieving that grade so we'll have to work really hard together, won't we."

Finally, the actual levels (or grades) that pupils achieve at the end of Key Stage 2 or 4 are compared with what the FFT data suggested the pupils could achieve. Results significantly above or below the expected are highlighted – green (light shaded in the version below) indicates above and bluer (dark shaded) indicates below. This is particularly helpful to senior leadership teams when discussing pupil attainment with their staff.

	Y2 Test Levels	Y2 TA Levels		Overall Estimate Actual	English Estimates Actual	Mathematics Estimates Actual	Science Estimates Actual
	RD WR MA	EN MA SC		Pts Pts	Lev L4+ L5+ Lev	Lev L4+ L5+ Lev	Lev L4+ L5+ Lev
Pupil A	3 3 3	3 3 3		32.5 33.1	5.2 99% 78% 5.2	5.6 99% 92% 5.7	5.5 99% 90% 5.7
Pupil B	3 3 3	3 3 3		31.7 33.8	5.0 99% 64% 5.6	5.4 99% 83% 5.6	5.5 99% 89% 5.7
Pupil C	2A 3 3	3 3 3		30.9 28.8	5.0 99% 64% 5.1	5.3 99% 76% 4.3	5.2 99% 75% 5.0
Pupil D	3 3 2A	3 2 2		30.0 30.4	5.0 99% 67% 5.2	4.8 96% 38% 5.3	5.1 98% 71% 4.6
Pupil E	2A 2B 3	2 3 2		29.2 32.8	4.6 96% 23% 5.2	5.0 97% 51% 5.6	5.0 97% 59% 5.6

Fischer Family Trust table showing results against estimates

The equivalent table for secondary schools shows for pupils at the end of Year 11:
- Year 6 Test and Teacher Assessment levels for English, Mathematics and Science
- Points – Estimated and Actual
- Number of A*-A Estimated and Actual
- Number of A*-C Estimated and Actual
- Number of A*-G Estimated and Actual
- Grades for English, Maths and Science Estimated and Actual

Pupils' attainment

While the progress pupils make relative to their starting points is important, the life chances of children and young people will be largely determined or at least influenced by the absolute measure of attainment. So governors can expect pupil attainment to be a key part of Ofsted's judgement and will be wise to do the analysis for themselves.

Any school can experience a blip in its results in a particular year – although the larger the school the less likely that it will be. So a strategic governing body will take less notice of changes from one year to another and ask instead: "Is the trend on an upward trajectory?" Graphs plot results over five years and include comparison with the national result so governors can see the long term trend. Inspectors are likely to make their judgements on the basis of three years' data.

Tables and bar graphs show the percentage of children achieving or exceeding particular levels at Key Stage 2. The table illustrated overleaf shows a school with fewer level 4 and many fewer Level 5s than the national average. The figures have been annotated by the author.

Evaluating your school's impact on pupil achievement

		A/T	<L3	L3+	L4+	L5+	
English	Entries	0	1	22	18	4	
	School	0	4	96	79	18	⎱ Low
	National	1	5	95	83	30	
	Difference	-1	0	0	-4	-12	
	Significance	-	-	-	-		
Mathematics	Entries	0	0	23	17	6	
	School	0	0	100	74	26	⎱ Better
	National	1	5	95	80	31	
	Difference	-1	-5	5	-6	-5	
	Significance	-	-	-	-		
Science	Entries	0	0	23	19	6	
	School	0	0	100	83	26	⎱ Very Low
	National	1	2	98	89	45	
	Difference	-1	-2	2	-7	-18	
	Significance	-	-	-	-		

Percentages of pupils attaining or surpassing each level at Key Stage 2

The equivalent tables for a secondary school would show pupils' attainment in the standard Key Stage 4 indicators over three years including the percentage of pupils attaining:

- 5+ grades A*-C,
- 5+ grades A*-C including English and Maths,
- 5+ A*-G including English and Maths,

and Average Points Score.

Another way to evaluate pupil attainment at your school is to compare Average Points Scores (APS) in primary and Capped Points Scores (CPS) in secondary with national figures. RAISEonline allows you to use APS and CPS scores to compare the attainment of your pupils from different ethnic groups with the national average. For example, the overall National APS for all National Curriculum Core Subjects for key stage 2 in 2011 was 27.5 while the national APS for the different ethnic groups ranged from 20.9 (Gypsy/Roma) to 29.7 (Chinese). When you look at your school's data you will be particularly anxious if the school's APS is below the national figure for a particular ethnic group – though for all groups you should want your school to do better than the national average.

When the data is not the whole picture

Governors are sometimes told that their school's circumstances, including high pupil mobility or an intake of pupils with particular difficulties, means that the data does not accurately reflect the school's impact on pupil achievement. You can substantiate that assertion by asking the leadership to produce a report with robust data and analysis, perhaps commissioned from an external consultant who will work alongside the headteacher.

Reading standards

Improving reading standards is a national priority. Governors should ask whether all children are at the expected reading levels in all age groups, and if not, what is being done about it. Ofsted inspectors will judge reading attainment by the end of Key Stage 1 and at the time they leave school.

> **Another bottom line**
>
> The government set a new floor standard for school performance in 2011. For both primary and secondary schools there are three measures. To be below the floor, a school has to fail to meet all three.
>
> For primary schools these have been set at:
>
> - 60 percent of pupils achieving at least level 4 in English and maths at Key Stage 2
> - the national average percentage of pupils making expected progress in English by the end of Key Stage 2 (the national median for 2010 is 87%)
> - the national average percentage of pupils making expected progress in maths by the end of Key Stage 2 (the national median for 2010 is 86%).
>
> "Expected progress" is an advance of two National Curriculum levels.
>
> For secondary schools the targets are:
>
> - 35 percent of pupils achieving at least five A*–C grade GCSEs, including English and maths
> - the national average percentage of pupils making expected progress in English between the ends of Key Stages 2 and 4 (national median for 2010 is 72%)
> - the national average percentage of pupils making expected progress in maths between the ends of Key Stages 2 and 4 (national median for 2010 is 65%).
>
> "Expected progress" is based on advancing from National Curriculum level 4 at the end of Key Stage 2 to at least a GCSE grade C, so also therefore from level 3 to an D grade, or level 5 to a B grade, etc.
>
> The floor standards are not immutable. The Secretary of State for Education has already (in June 2011) announced that he will increase the first secondary-school floor target to 40 percent in 2013 and possibly to 50 percent in 2015.

Special needs

These elements appear in the evaluation of achievement:

- How well disabled pupils and those with SEN have achieved since joining the school.
- How well gaps are narrowing between children with different levels of SEN and those without, and compared to all pupils nationally.

In September 2010 Ofsted inspectors were asked to shine a particularly strong light on the impact of each school's provision for pupils with special educational needs. Ofsted's concern was prompted by looking at the finance – spending on SEN had increased in the past seven years from c.£2.8 billion to c.£4.9 billion – and by social factors: research published under the title *Getting a Life* found that the employment chances of young people with SEN are limited, while a KPMG report in 2006 cites a significant correlation between poor educational outcomes and poor health outcomes such as depression, obesity, respiratory problems and lack of exercise.

There may be some wonderful work that addresses the needs of pupils with SEN in your school. Asking questions about the aspects which Ofsted has expressed concerns about will give your headteacher and SENCO the opportunity to report on your school's strengths. It will also give your school an opportunity to address aspects which are not as good as they could be.

> **Ofsted's description of good pupil achievement**
> Pupils are making better progress than all pupils nationally given their starting points. Groups of pupils, including disabled pupils and those with special educational needs, are also making better progress than similar groups of pupils nationally. Performance will exceed floor standards. Pupils acquire knowledge quickly and are secure in their understanding in different subjects. They develop and apply a range of skills well, including reading, writing, communication and mathematical skills, across the curriculum that will ensure they are well prepared for the next stage in their education, training or employment. The standards of attainment of the large majority of groups of pupils are likely to be at least in line with national averages for all pupils. Where standards of any group of pupils are below those of all pupils nationally, the gaps are closing. In exceptional circumstances, where attainment, including attainment in reading in primary schools, is low overall, it is improving at a faster rate than nationally over a sustained period.

Interventions are meant to lead to pupils making faster progress so that they can catch up. Governor evaluation should include asking the school to produce evidence to show the impact of interventions; including children removed from the SEN register as a result of successful support. Helping school leaders to reflect on what works best will enable schools to make better decisions and to drop strategies that are of only marginal value.

Special schools

Many special schools have less robust local and national benchmarking data on pupil attainment and progress than mainstream schools. Some pupils will not have reached Level 1. For those pupils, "P scales" are used to demonstrate small but often significant steps in their progress. For others, the school may need to use modified mainstream measures.

From whatever level pupils start, schools will expect to demonstrate good progress. This requires consistent assessment of levels attained and accurate recording so that individual pupils' progress can be tracked, success celebrated, and strategies put in place where difficulties are identified.

Governors should ask about their school's procedures for moderating attainment levels and whether they involve staff from outside the school. The local authority may have data which enables the achievement of pupils with similar learning needs and common profiles of past performance to be compared across special and mainstream schools. Moreover, the school may take the initiative in collaborating with one or more similar schools – not necessarily in the same authority – to look at each other's data and the systems that have produced it.

The following note in Ofsted's 2012 Evaluation Schedule particularly relates to special schools:

> "While many pupils with special educational needs are not precluded from attaining as well as or better than their peers, for those groups of pupils whose cognitive ability is such that their attainment is unlikely ever to rise above 'low', the judgement on achievement should be based on an evaluation of the pupils' learning and progress relative to their starting points at particular ages and any assessment measures held by the school, but should not take account of their attainment compared to national benchmarks."

3 How effective is teaching?

"At the heart of every learning institution is good teaching, with a clear focus by the organisation's leadership on continually improving teaching, which leads in turn to consistently high standards of practice by teachers. However, the quality of teaching is still too variable: too much is satisfactory and too little outstanding teaching was seen … Satisfactory teaching does not deliver good enough progress for pupils in the most challenging circumstances … Our new school inspection framework will focus more attention on this issue: it is a priority for improvement across the school system."

Ofsted Annual Report 2010/11

There was a time when the quality of teaching was thought to mean how well a teacher performed in lessons observed by inspectors and/or the school's leaders. However, for many years now Ofsted has required inspectors to take into account pupil outcomes, evidence of assessment and planning over time and the evidence of work in pupils' books.

Ofsted's 2010/11 Annual Report describes three elements of outstanding teaching:

1. Lessons planned, structured and executed with high expectations
2. Quality of dialogue and interaction including expert explanation, judicious questioning and giving time for pupils to explore questions and solve problems
3. Quality of assessment to inform planning, differentiation and feedback before lessons, during the lesson to check understanding and change course when necessary.

Governors are not in a position to have a direct impact on improving teaching, but you do have the overall responsibility for ensuring that teaching is as good as it can be. By focusing school self-evaluation on teaching quality you can create the conditions in which senior leaders are encouraged to communicate to all staff a route to improvement. There will not be many schools that can say, "We don't need to improve teaching." On the contrary, the schools with outstanding teaching who might be thought justified in saying "We can't improve" will be the very ones that are pushing for even more improvement.

The governing body's greatest contribution to improving teaching lies in setting the right agenda

Below the bottom line – Ofsted's description of inadequate

Teaching is likely to be inadequate where any of the following apply:

- As a result of weak teaching over time pupils or groups of pupils currently in the school are making inadequate progress.
- Teachers do not have sufficiently high expectations and teaching over time fails to excite, enthuse, engage or motivate particular groups of pupils, including disabled pupils and those who have special educational needs.
- Pupils cannot communicate, read, write or use mathematics as well as they should.
- Learning activities are not sufficiently well matched to the needs of pupils so that they make inadequate progress.

for its work and a schedule of the information it requires. Ofsted's 2012 Evaluation Schedule indicates to governing bodies the information they should be seeking. The order in which they will ask for it and the way it is collected is likely to be affected by the school's circumstances, so you need to take into account – but not unquestioningly accept – the advice of the headteacher.

You will get some idea of the effectiveness of teaching by looking at SATs or exam results for all pupils, and at results for specific groups of pupils, such as those with SEN and/or disabilities, those entitled to free school meals (FSM), those with English as an Additional Language (EAL), and the more able pupils. You should look separately at the levels pupils have attained in reading, writing, communication and mathematics. Other factors may have come into play, but the outcomes will have been significantly affected by teaching quality. Beyond looking at these results, you are going to be dependent on the information you ask for and get from the headteacher and/or other members of the senior leadership.

The three elements of outstanding teaching listed in the Ofsted report provide a good framework for grouping the points in the Evaluation Schedule that explore the effectiveness of teaching.

Lessons planned, structured and executed with high expectations

Inspectors will consider:

- the extent to which teachers' expectations, reflected in their teaching and planning, including curriculum planning, are sufficiently high to extend the previous knowledge, skills and understanding of all pupils in a range of lessons and activities over time

- the quality of teaching and other support provided for pupils with a range of aptitudes and needs, including for those with special educational needs and/or disabilities, so that their learning improves

- the extent to which teachers enable pupils to develop the skills to learn for themselves, where appropriate, including setting appropriate homework to develop their understanding.

You should ask how long-term planning converts to classroom practice. Good teaching will be evident in well-paced lessons that use a range of resources and activities, which support and challenge all pupils, and which make imaginative and effective use of the internet, technology and homework to involve pupils in learning for themselves. You should be able to find out how effectively these are being done from reports by the headteacher and/or other senior leaders that summarise the findings of their lesson observations, monitoring of planning and book scrutiny of pupils' work. The details are not appropriate: you should not ask for information on particular teachers as this is only for the senior leadership team, but you would want to be assured that lesson observations are rigorous and understand what the overall picture shows.

You may suggest that some of this observation and monitoring is conducted with or by an outside professional such as an adviser or a senior leader from another school. It is excellent professional development to see how staff operate in different schools and it helps teachers to get used to showing and explaining their practice to an outsider.

It is important to know that planning includes effective differentiation for pupils with identified needs, such as those listed earlier in this chapter. If there are additional staff in the classroom, senior leaders should be satisfied that they have a good understanding of the lesson plan and are clear about their role in implementing it. A staff questionnaire may provide another perspective and show you the circumstances in which adult support works well, together with their ideas for further development and training needs.

The use of support staff in classrooms is particularly important when it comes to support of children with SEN. These children need teachers' time but in some schools too much work with them is delegated to teaching assistants (TAs). Research from the Institute of Education in London University, *Deployment and Impact of Support Staff in Schools* (2009), found – unsurprisingly – that teachers were better than TAs at explaining concepts, using prompts to help pupils to answer and using feedback to encourage learning. TAs' explanations were more likely to be inaccurate or confusing; they were more likely to supply answers and were more often task-orientated. You may want to ask how well-trained the school's TAs are and how are they deployed. Do they have a clear idea of the lesson plan and how they will adapt materials, explanations and questions to support one or more pupils' learning? Are they always expected to work with children with SEN, with the result that these pupils are largely ignored by teachers?

Children need to learn independence so they can operate increasingly confidently without enhanced support. Those with an adult stuck by their side throughout the lesson will, on the contrary, be learning to be dependent. You can ask for reports on the strategies to help them acquire attitudes and skills that lead to their greater independence, such as using their initiative.

Teachers should be planning opportunities for all pupils to learn for themselves. The report from the headteacher could contain an analysis of the range of strategies included in planning and observed in lessons that encourage pupils to find things out for themselves, whether in class or as part of homework. You should ensure that your homework policy is adequate and clarifies what homework is expected to achieve. It might be instructive to survey pupils and parents about their perceptions of homework.

Homework survey questions

Governors can obtain information on homework and involve parents and carers in their child's education by carrying out a brief parent survey.

What do you think is the main reason for giving homework to pupils in this Year group?:
Tick up to three of the statements below

(a) to finish work not completed in lessons

(b) to get pupils used to working independently

(c) to get parents involved

(d) to show parents the sort of work their child can do

(e) to give children a chance to practice reading and writing

(f) to revise for tests.

Do you help your child with his/her homework? YES/NO

If yes, what sort of things do you do?

How regularly does your child receive homework?

Do you think this is more or less than school policy?

Any other comments....

Quality of dialogue and interaction including expert explanation, judicious questioning and giving time for pupils to explore questions and solve problems

Inspectors will consider:

- the extent to which well judged and effective teaching strategies successfully engage pupils in their learning
- the extent to which teachers secure high quality learning by setting challenging tasks that are matched to pupils' specific learning needs
- the extent to which teachers' questioning and use of discussion promote learning
- how well teachers use their expertise, including their subject knowledge, to develop pupils' knowledge, skills and understanding across a range of subjects and areas of learning
- the extent to which teachers enthuse, engage and motivate pupils to learn and foster their curiosity and enthusiasm for learning.

Reports from senior leaders, again, will be the most important way in which you can get to know the quality of dialogue. This may be through lesson observations, with examples of particularly effective activities which have enthused and motivated pupils and of really effective questioning and challenging differentiation. Where there is less effective teaching it may include an analysis of how long teachers talk at the class, giving insufficient time for pupils to communicate what they do and do not understand, to work independently and to use their initiative. (One school's answer to this problem was to give every teacher a kitchen timer – but that is an operational decision!)

In all cases the report on lesson observations could be followed by a list of actions that the school is taking to consolidate strengths and address weaknesses. It might include a record of staff discussion where staff have described a range of strategies that have worked well in different circumstances and which are appropriate for different learning needs. The Ofsted Annual Report

> **Ofsted's description of outstanding teaching**
> Much of the teaching in all key stages and most subjects is outstanding and never less than consistently good. As a result, almost all pupils are making rapid and sustained progress. All teachers have consistently high expectations of all pupils. Drawing on excellent subject knowledge, teachers plan astutely and set challenging tasks based on systematic, accurate assessment of pupils' prior skills, knowledge and understanding. They use well judged and often imaginative teaching strategies that, together with sharply focused and timely support and intervention, match individual needs accurately. Consequently, pupils learn exceptionally well across the curriculum. The teaching of reading, writing, communication and mathematics is highly effective. Teachers and other adults generate high levels of enthusiasm for, participation in and commitment to learning. Teaching promotes pupils' high levels of resilience, confidence and independence when they tackle challenging activities. Teachers systematically and effectively check pupils' understanding throughout lessons, anticipating where they may need to intervene and doing so with notable impact on the quality of learning. Time is used very well and every opportunity is taken to successfully develop crucial skills, including being able to use their literacy and numeracy skills in other subjects. Appropriate and regular homework contributes very well to pupils' learning. Marking and constructive feedback from teachers and pupils are frequent and of a consistently high quality, leading to high levels of engagement and interest.

described some outstanding examples of teachers using their expertise to "explain things clearly, anticipate pupils' misconceptions, select their teaching strategies judiciously, and target the use of high quality questioning so that all pupils are involved and understanding is developed".

Sometimes when there is a weakness it stems from insecure subject knowledge. This may occur because of the breadth of the curriculum a teacher has to deliver in primary schools, or because shortage subjects in a secondary school have required a teacher to operate outside their usual area of knowledge. Where there is weak subject knowledge teachers may give explanations and responses which add little to pupils' understanding. If this looks like a possibility, ask the headteacher if it is so, and request an analysis of the issue, a description of what steps have been taken to address identified gaps – including training and recruitment – how successful these have been, and what more needs to be done. It may be appropriate to seek advice and support from another school. Pupil surveys or focus groups can also be revealing here.

Quality of assessment to inform planning, differentiation and feedback before lessons, during the lesson to check understanding and change course when necessary

Inspectors will consider:

- the extent to which teachers' expectations, reflected in their teaching and planning, including curriculum planning, are sufficiently high to extend the previous knowledge, skills and understanding of all pupils in a range of lessons and activities over time

- the extent to which the pace and depth of learning are maximised as a result of teachers' monitoring of learning during lessons and any consequent actions in response to pupils' feedback

- how well pupils understand how to improve their learning as a result of frequent, detailed and accurate feedback from teachers following assessment of their learning.

Planning to provide challenge must start with an accurate assessment of how far each child has reached in their learning. If this is not accurate a teacher's plans to meet the needs of the variety

---

Examples of questions to ask in a pupil survey
How well do you think you learn when:

    I listen to the teacher introducing the lesson

    I work on my own in the classroom

    I work on my own doing homework

    I work with a group of other pupils with no adult

    I work with a group of pupils and the teacher

    I work with a group of other pupils and another adult

    I take part in teacher questioning and pupil discussion during the lesson

(Ask pupils to grade their answers on a scale ranging from "not at all" to "very well".)

Give five examples of exciting learning activities your teacher has done with you in the last month.

What was the most useful/interesting/exciting piece of homework you were given in the past month? Can you explain why?

of children in their class will not be effective. Ofsted has noted that too often, especially in secondary schools, teachers identify progress to be made by different ability groups but "do nothing different for these groups and simply rely on students to make the expected progress, based on their prior attainment". That is no way to narrow the gap.

The Ofsted Annual Report 2010/11 says of assessment: "Assessment that clearly identifies pupils' starting points and understanding, checks progress, establishes what has been learnt and can inform the next steps in learning is at the core of good and outstanding teaching. Effective assessment within lessons enables pupils to demonstrate their understanding and ensures that teachers can adapt their teaching in real time to the needs of the pupils." The report also points out teachers assume too often that because one pupil has answered a question correctly the whole class understands.

So how can you discover how effectively assessment is used across your school? Again, you will mainly be dependent on reports from senior leaders with corroboration from external consultants and/or other schools. You need not only to ask the question but also what the evidence is, if necessary encouraging the head to seek evidence on aspects that have not been previously considered. You might ask for the report to contain examples of where lessons have departed from the teacher's plan as a result of in-class assessment which has either revealed that a large group have misunderstood a key concept or that they have clearly grasped the lesson objective and are ready to move on.

Quality of teaching in the Early Years Foundation Stage

While evaluation of this aspect of primary schools will be subsumed into the whole school it is important to recognise the distinctive features of teaching the youngest children. The Ofsted Annual Report notes that nursery schools have the highest proportion of outstanding teaching of any schools. This may be because teachers can get to know the children well and what they need to learn. For younger children especially, the best classrooms are exciting environments which exhibit imaginative approaches to learning to capture children's enthusiasm, and outside play areas are just as exciting. Inside and out the learning resources are of high quality and are easily accessible so that children are encouraged to make choices. Signs that senior managers should watch are disorganised areas where planning is not evident, children are distracted by irrelevant clutter and good, appropriate resources are hard to find.

Governor visits

So, where do governor visits fit into obtaining evidence on the effectiveness of teaching for school self-evaluation? You are not an inspector and it is the headteacher and senior leaders who must remain responsible for making professional judgements. But if you visit school with the clear intention to learn how different parts of the school operate, you will not only improve your own and your fellow governors' understanding but also help staff to improve their own practice.

The National College has found clear evidence of the significant improvement in their own practice when good and outstanding teachers explain their methods to other teachers. In the same way, when teachers take time to explain their practice to an interested governor they will clarify why they do what they do and that will aid their own improvement. The trick for you as a governor is to go into the visit to listen and learn, to ask clarifying rather than challenging questions, to thank the teacher and to reserve discussion of any concerns you may have to a time when you can talk to the headteacher.

What to do about concerns

In the course of considering reports you may discern a pattern where quality is less good in some subjects or certain year groups or classes. If so, it is possible that there is a capability issue. This would be the headteacher's job to address. Governors must keep out of the way – apart from the chair of governors who, as sounding board for the head, may know a little about it – because if the concern were to end in a dismissal the governing body would need to be able to form two panels of governors (one to deal with the dismissal and the other to hear any appeal) who have no previous knowledge of the case.

You can ask in general terms about the process for the head to address capability and should be assured that it starts with setting targets for improvement and providing support to give the staff member every chance of achieving the targets. If the teaching standard is not such as to be a capability issue there will certainly need to be a systematic development programme.

Another source of the problem might be the allocation of teachers. There's no school where all the teachers will be of the same quality in all aspects of their work. In looking at primary schools the Ofsted Annual Report 2010/11 noted that there is "a tendency for schools to focus strongly on positioning the best teaching at the end of each key stage. This approach runs the risk that progress can dip in the intervening years, with too much satisfactory teaching in Years 1, 3 and 4 in particular." While staff deployment is a matter for the headteacher, you are certainly entitled to ask about this if you think it is happening in your school.

The last point that Ofsted looks at under quality of assessment is "how well teaching enables pupils to develop skills in reading, writing, communication and mathematics". This was covered in chapter 2, on achievement.

Ofsted's description of good teaching

As a result of teaching that is mainly good, with examples of outstanding teaching, most pupils and groups of pupils, including disabled pupils and those who have special educational needs, are achieving well over time. Teachers have high expectations of all pupils. Teachers in most subjects and key stages use their well developed subject knowledge and their accurate assessment of pupils' prior skills, knowledge and understanding to plan effectively and set challenging tasks. They use effective teaching strategies that, together with appropriately targeted support and intervention, match most pupils' individual needs so that pupils learn well across the curriculum. The teaching of reading, writing, communication and mathematics is very efficient. Teachers and other adults enthuse and motivate most pupils to participate. Teaching generally promotes pupils' resilience, confidence and independence when tackling challenging activities. Teachers regularly listen astutely to, carefully observe and skilfully question groups of pupils and individuals during lessons in order to reshape tasks and explanations to improve learning. Teaching consistently deepens pupils' knowledge and understanding and allows them to develop a range of skills including communication, reading and writing, and mathematics across the curriculum. Appropriate and regular homework contributes well to pupils' learning. Teachers assess pupils' progress regularly and accurately and discuss assessments with them so that pupils know how well they have done and what they need to do to improve.

4 Behaviour and safety

"Where behaviour is poor, the quality of teaching is also likely to be poor. Where teaching does not meet pupils' needs or does not engage pupils sufficiently they can lose attention, demonstrate poor attitudes to learning and eventually interrupt the learning of others. In these cases teaching can then focus too much on continually managing low-level disruption at the expense of providing interesting and relevant opportunities for pupils to learn. Poor behaviour also makes it difficult to teach well."

Ofsted Annual Report 2010/11

The Ofsted Inspection Framework operative since January 2012 says:

"When evaluating the behaviour and safety of pupils at the school, inspectors will consider:

- pupils' attitudes to learning and conduct in lessons and around the school
- pupils' behaviour towards, and respect for, other young people and adults, including freedom from bullying and harassment that may include cyber-bullying and prejudice-based bullying related to special educational need, sexual orientation, sex, race, religion and belief, gender reassignment or disability
- how well teachers manage the behaviour and expectations of pupils to ensure that all pupils have an equal and fair chance to thrive and learn in an atmosphere of respect and dignity
- pupils' ability to assess and manage risk appropriately and to keep themselves safe
- pupils' attendance and punctuality at school and in lessons
- how well the school ensures the systematic and consistent management of behaviour.

Below the bottom line – Ofsted's description of inadequate
Behaviour and safety are likely to be inadequate when any of the following apply.

- Parents, carers, pupils or staff raise major and/or well founded concerns about behaviour that are not being addressed.
- Pupils' lack of engagement and persistent low-level disruption contribute more than occasionally to reduced learning and/or a disorderly classroom environment.
- A significant minority of pupils show a lack of respect and intolerance for each other or staff and a lack of self-discipline, resulting in poor behaviour around the school.
- Incidents of bullying overall or specific types of bullying including cyber-bullying and prejudice-based bullying related to special educational need, sexual orientation, sex, race, religion and belief, gender reassignment or disability, are frequent or pupils have little confidence in the school's ability to address bullying successfully.
- Pupils or specific groups of pupils do not feel safe.
- Attendance is consistently low for all pupils or groups of pupils and shows little or no sign of improvement.

Pupils' attitudes to learning and conduct in lessons and around the school

Staff should be able to analyse the evidence indicating pupils' respect for and courtesy towards each other and adults, and their care for school facilities as shown by their behaviour around the school, and produce a report on these for governors. Pupil perceptions would be helpful here. You could ask the headteacher to work with their colleagues to produce an analysis of pupil attitudes to learning in a range of different learning groups and settings. Are there particular year groups or subjects where behaviour is better than average – and what factors might explain that? Can those insights be used to improve attitudes and behaviour elsewhere? Do pupils behave the same with support and administrative staff, with new, inexperienced staff and with supply teachers? If not, what can the school do about it? It might be instructive to compare staff perceptions with those of students, collected through questionnaires or discussion, for example, with the School Council.

This is an instance where useful evidence can also be obtained from a series of governor visits. You might make a point of observing the way pupils treat others – including you as the visiting governor. You could note the way pupils move around the school in breaks and between lessons, and particularly how they behave at crowded pinch points. The amount of litter and graffiti indicate how they care for their school. If there are problems the governing body could ask the headteacher to consider strategies to promote cohesion within the school community, changes to smarten up the school site, and action to clear litter and clean off graffiti quickly.

An external view can be very revealing. You could ask neighbours and local shopkeepers – the local corner shop is a useful source – about the behaviour of pupils. This would not only provide useful data and indicate possible improvements but demonstrate to neighbours that the governing body cares.

Pupils' behaviour towards, and respect for, other young people and adults, including freedom from bullying and harassment that may include cyber-bullying and prejudice-based bullying related to special educational need, sexual orientation, sex, race, religion and belief, gender reassignment or disability

If you have been working to establish a school culture and ethos that promote positive attitudes towards disabled people and celebrate cultural differences, you will want to measure the impact of this. If you have pupils with disabilities in your school, is there evidence that they are treated by other pupils in a fairly matter-of-fact and supportive manner? And does a similar outlook show through in pupils' interaction with peers who have special educational needs or any other form of difficulty? Is there a substantial willingness to enquire about cultural or religious difference and to share different ideas and experience? These are all rather nebulous things which staff who are in school all the time may be able to describe to governors. Statistical evidence will be harder to obtain, but carrying out attitude surveys through questionnaires and focus group discussions may provide some firm evidence; you could commission professionals to conduct these.

Bullying is an area that every governing body will want to measure and analyse at some time because no school is entirely free from it. Alarm bells should ring inside your head if you are told that "there's no bullying here". Such a statement is likely to reflect a lack of awareness of the issue or a tendency to dismiss all incidents as "innocent horse-play". Evaluating this will become a priority if you become aware of parental concerns. You need to be assured that your school's anti-bullying policy is being implemented consistently and that it is working effectively.

You should ask your headteacher to report on the number and nature of incidents of bullying and how different types or levels of bullying are handled. You should not ask for details of specific incidents, but you should be shown the pattern of them. If the headteacher cannot easily produce an analysis this indicates poor record-keeping that needs to be remedied very quickly.

The most useful reports will look back to previous years and compare the pattern of incidents. This will provide evidence of how effective any actions to prevent and tackle bullying have been. If the number of incidents has risen in the short term it may be an indication of better systems, but you would then expect the frequency to decline, and if it doesn't you should be questioning whether the school should be doing more or something different. The pattern may change as new forms of harassment become possible. For example, a few years ago cyber-bullying using mobile phones and social networks was unknown but is now quite common. New forms of bullying like this call for new strategies to deal with them.

Under the Equality Act 2010 the school has a duty to address prejudice-based bullying – including name-calling. So any record keeping must note if there is a possibility that bullying or harassment is related to any of the "protected characteristics" listed above. Schools have a duty to do what they can to prevent these, which involves education as much as rules and sanctions.

Pupil questionnaires should include questions about their experience of bullying. If they reveal a significant problem there needs to be further analysis, to be explored by staff with groups of pupils – the School Council, for example. Pupils need to feel confident that they can talk about any type of bullying, including that based on prejudice, which may raise very sensitive issues for the victim. The school may also seek the views of parents and carers as they may know about the bullying experienced by their children and the effect it has had on them at home.

How well teachers manage the behaviour and expectations of pupils to ensure that all pupils have an equal and fair chance to thrive and learn in an atmosphere of respect and dignity

and

How well the school ensures the systematic and consistent management of behaviour

What counts is not so much the fact that pupils' behaviour sometimes falls below the standard that schools set, but the frequency with which that happens and the way that it is handled. If you have asked the headteacher for a report on behaviour it should include the school's response to poor behaviour in lessons over time – for example, analysis of incident logs so a pattern of the type and severity of behaviour can be seen. Year-by-year (or in some cases term-by-term) analyses will show whether the severity and frequency of behaviour incidents is changing.

Check whether any particular groups of children are heavily represented in this analysis and, if so, ask for the reasons why. The school must not be acting in a way that is discriminatory, even if it is quite unintentional.

The number of exclusions, both fixed-term and permanent, is an indication of the level of poor behaviour in the school. Does the pattern of exclusions show a significant increase or decrease over the years? If there are a lot of exclusions, does this indicate that behaviour problems are not being dealt with early enough or firmly enough? Are teachers taking a consistent approach, or is behaviour that is acceptable in one class regarded as unacceptable in another?

Is the school taking account of pupils' special educational needs and/or disabilities when handling behaviour issues? Children with statements of SEN are eight times more likely to be permanently excluded than the rest of children. Children with SEN but no statement are nine and a half times more likely to be permanently excluded than the rest. If certain behaviour is a characteristic of a particular need or disability, the school should be making reasonable adjustments. If there is a

> **Ofsted's description of outstanding behaviour and safety**
> Parents, carers, staff and pupils are highly positive about behaviour and safety. Pupils make an exceptional contribution to a safe, positive learning environment. They make every effort to ensure that others learn and thrive in an atmosphere of respect and dignity. Pupils show very high levels of engagement, courtesy, collaboration and cooperation in and out of lessons. They have excellent, enthusiastic attitudes to learning, enabling lessons to proceed without interruption. Pupils are consistently punctual in arriving at school and lessons. They are highly adept at managing their own behaviour in the classroom and in social situations, supported by systematic, consistently applied approaches to behaviour management. They are very calm, orderly and considerate when moving around the school. There are excellent improvements in behaviour over time for any individuals or groups with particular behavioural difficulties. Instances of bullying, including cyber-bullying and prejudice-based bullying related to special educational need, sexual orientation, sex, race, religion and belief, gender reassignment or disability are extremely rare. Pupils are acutely aware of different forms of bullying and actively try to prevent it from occurring. The school has an active and highly effective approach to identifying and tackling bullying. All groups of pupils feel safe at school at all times. They understand very clearly what constitutes unsafe situations and are highly aware of how to keep themselves and others safe. It is likely that attendance will be above average for all groups of pupils or will show sustained and convincing improvement over time.

high incidence of exclusions of statemented pupils it may indicate that the school is not meeting its obligations to those pupils.

Schools have a responsibility to provide meaningful work for excluded pupils to do at home. Is there evidence that this duty is being met and that pupils are well-supported for return after a fixed-term exclusion? If not, this is likely to perpetuate poor behaviour by making a pupil feel they are branded as "bad". It may be appropriate to conduct a survey of excluded pupils and their parents/carers to check how the school's systems are perceived from the other side. You may need to revise the school's behaviour policy after this.

The school may have taken a range of actions to improve behaviour, for example by improving teaching, introducing a rewards system, or applying more consistent sanctions. The analysis should demonstrate where the action has had the intended impact, where it has failed to achieve the improvement expected (and further change is required) or where the initiative simply needs more time.

Inspectors are now alert to the possibility that the behaviour they see may be affected by some of the worst behaved pupils being out of school while the inspection is taking place. That is one reason why inspectors are asked to consider whether the behaviour they see is typical. They may do this by asking pupils, or looking at an attendance register and asking to see the file for a few pupils not in school.

Inspectors may conduct case studies to evaluate the experience of particular individuals and groups, including pupils with special educational needs and/or disabilities, looked after children and those with mental health needs. You could ask the school to talk you through one or more case studies of this nature. Rehearsing in this way may help to highlight issues that the school needs to address.

Pupils' ability to assess and manage risk appropriately and keep themselves safe

However safe schools manage to make their own environment, pupils are confronted with a range of risks in their school lives and will also need to be equipped to deal with them in the future. Part of education is learning to understand and respond to risk. You can ask the headteacher to explain when and how pupils are helped to learn how to cope with common risks and threats:

- to act safely around roads and railways, water and fire
- to understand the dangers of substance misuse, knives, gangs and extremism, and have strategies for avoiding them
- to navigate relationships (including sexual relationships) and avoid contact with inappropriate people through the internet.

A secondary school might judge its effectiveness by looking at the effect of its stay-safe strategies on former students. It is a sad fact, for example, that serious and sometimes fatal car accidents are a consequence of risky behaviour of young adults, especially males.

Pupils' attendance and punctuality at school and in lessons

Pupil attendance is a key aspect of pupil behaviour. Being in school regularly is a pre-condition of being able to learn and, at least in older children, gives an indication of pupils' attitude to learning. You need to know how your school's overall absence compares with national averages over the last three years.

The guidance to inspectors on judging attendance for many years has used the percentages in the table below.

Attendance rated	Primary	Secondary
High	Above 96%	94% or above
Above average	95.1% – 96%	92.4% – 93.9%
Average	94% – 95%	91.7% – 92.3%
Low	Below 94%	Below 91.6%

You can expect your headteacher and colleagues to have analysed attendance patterns for different groups. If attendance is high or above average, this issue is unlikely to be a priority. But otherwise, the analysis might help to explain why outcomes are not yet good, and this might indicate a fruitful strategy for improvement. You might ask what actions the school takes to improve attendance. There may be particular initiatives you might support or suggest, such as appointing a home-school liaison officer.

Governors should also ask about punctuality – both at the start of school sessions and at lesson changeover. Lateness disrupts learning for all, while punctuality is a useful life skill and is essential in the world of work. Many schools find that breakfast clubs have a positive effect on attendance and punctuality and help to give some pupils the energy for learning.

The difficulties that children with special educational needs experience at school seems to find expression for some pupils in persistent absence. The percentage of pupils with SEN and/or Disability (SEND) who are persistently absent is 9.8 compared with 3.6 for non-SEND children (October 2009). An analysis of you school's absence figures will show whether a similar pattern applies in your school. If so, what is the school doing to address this; and if not, what are we doing right?

> **Ofsted's description of good behaviour and safety**
> There are few well founded concerns expressed by parents, carers, staff and pupils about behaviour and safety. Pupils are typically considerate, respectful and courteous to staff and each other and consistently meet the school's expectations. This makes a very positive contribution to a well ordered, safe school. The very large majority of pupils are consistently punctual to school and to lessons. In lessons, pupils demonstrate positive attitudes towards the teacher, their learning and each other. Their good levels of engagement allow lessons to flow smoothly throughout so that disruption is unusual. Pupils, including those with identified behavioural difficulties, respond very well to the school's strategies for managing and improving behaviour, which are applied consistently. Disruptive incidents seldom occur. There are marked improvements in behaviour over time for individuals or groups with particular needs. Instances of bullying, including cyber-bullying and prejudice-based bullying related to special educational need, sexual orientation, sex, race, religion and belief, gender reassignment or disability, are rare. Pupils have a good awareness of different forms of bullying and take active steps to prevent it from occurring. The school swiftly and successfully addresses any incidents of bullying that do occur, thus gaining the full confidence of pupils, parents and carers. Pupils feel safe at school. They understand clearly what constitutes unsafe situations and how to keep themselves safe. Where pupils are able to influence their own attendance, it is likely that attendance will be above average for all sizeable groups of pupils, or showing sustained and convincing improvement over time.

Reminder: The planning grid on page 50 allows you to record the judgements for your school in each area together with your improvement priorities and the focus for further evaluation.

5 Leadership and management

The Inspection Evaluation Schedule states:

> "What inspectors look for when judging leadership and management is the extent to which leaders and managers at all levels including, where relevant, governors:
> - demonstrate an ambitious vision for the school and high expectations for what every pupil and teacher can achieve, and set high standards for quality and performance
> - improve teaching and learning including the management of pupils' behaviour
> - provide a broad and balanced curriculum that meets the needs of all pupils, enables all pupils to achieve their full educational potential and make progress in their learning, and that promotes their good behaviour and safety and their spiritual, moral, social and cultural development
> - evaluate the school's strengths and weaknesses and use their findings to promote improvement
> - improve the school and develop its capacity for sustaining improvement by developing leadership capacity and high professional standards among all staff
> - engage with parents and carers in supporting pupils' achievement, behaviour and safety and their spiritual, moral, social and cultural development
> - ensure that all pupils are safe."

The other reference to governing bodies in the Evaluation Schedule appears in the guidance for inspectors to consider "effective work by the governing body that acts as a critical friend and holds senior leaders to account for all aspects of the school's performance". Your own performance ought to contribute strength to the school's leadership. This will be considered later.

> **Below the bottom line – Ofsted's description of inadequate**
> Leadership and management are likely to be inadequate if any of the following apply:
> - Capacity for further improvement is limited because current leaders and managers have been ineffective in securing essential improvements since the last inspection.
> - Leaders and managers are not taking effective steps to secure satisfactory and better teaching for all groups of pupils, including disabled pupils and those who have special educational needs.
> - The curriculum fails to meet the needs of pupils or particular groups of pupils.
> - Despite remedying a few small areas of weakness, perhaps recently, improvements are fragile, too slow or depend on external support.
> - The school's strategies for engaging with parents and carers are weak so that parents and carers are not involved sufficiently in supporting their children's learning and development.
> - The school's arrangements for safeguarding pupils do not meet statutory requirements and give serious cause for concern.

Demonstrate an ambitious vision for the school and high expectations for what every pupil and teacher can achieve, and set high standards for quality and performance

The Evaluation Schedule expects leaders and managers to be "relentless" and "rigorous" in pursuit of school improvement, to engage pupils, parents and staff in realising their vision and to develop leadership capacity and high professional standards among staff

Governing bodies should review all the evidence they have already seen on pupil achievement and behaviour to evaluate how well school leaders and managers enable pupils to overcome specific barriers to learning and promote improvements for all pupils and groups of pupils. You should be asking yourself:

- Is there evidence across the school of an ambitious shared vision and high expectations?
- How well have priorities for school improvement been identified to focus on the things that will really make a difference in the school?
- Have plans been implemented rigorously, monitored by senior leaders and clearly reported to the governing body?
- Have the changes brought about by these plans had a positive impact, especially on specific groups?
- Looking back at the previous inspection report, can you point to evidence that the key issues in that report have been energetically and effectively addressed?
- Has the school moved on to address other issues, or is the school leadership (including the governing body) only galvanised by the prospect of the next inspection?

One of the things that holds back school improvement is where policies and procedures, however well judged, are not consistently applied across the school. This may be a result of poor communication, including a lack of reminders, or because practical difficulties in implementation have not been identified and addressed or because inadequate monitoring makes staff believe the issue is not important. By identifying the most important policies for the school's current situation and asking the headteacher to report on the way they are being implemented, you can help school management to motivate staff if necessary.

The importance of parent and carer support to the school is huge. An effective governing body will have been involved in working with senior leaders to explain what the school is trying to achieve and how parents and carers can help. You may already have discussed strategies for getting to the "hard to reach" groups whose involvement may well have the greatest effect. Ask the questions "What is the evidence that parents understand and contribute to our key aims and vision?" and "Is there anything more we should be trying to do in order to harness their energies?". You can acquire evidence from questionnaires and/or focus groups, from the attendance of parents at open evenings, and from the liveliness of the PTA. Information from the headteacher's report on the number of challenges to the use of sanctions can also provide evidence.

Similar questions could be asked of staff and pupils. Have priorities and school improvement been discussed with staff? How clearly do they understand the vision and the contribution that they are expected to make? The School Council can be the channel through which pupils convey their thoughts on improvement and where pupil understanding of the priorities is gauged and messages about school vision are refined. If there is not already a governor who liaises with the School Council, the governing body can ask for an invitation to some of its meetings so as to hear from pupils first hand. You might ask the School Council to conduct a survey of pupil views or might organise the survey yourselves, taking care to ensure that the views of particular groups are heard.

Governing bodies need only reflect on their discussions with the headteacher and senior staff over the past year to judge whether they have high expectations about securing improvement. Is this reflected by challenging targets, or are targets firmly in the school's comfort zone? A proposal that from September 2012 inspectors should ask to see an anonymised analysis of staff performance management objectives may reveal that schools stuck on "satisfactory" have not used the performance management of senior leaders to address the problem.

How well those expectations are communicated to staff may be more difficult to judge, but it can probably be sensed by governors in their level of enthusiasm. You will be aware of the rigour of monitoring from the evidence the headteacher provides on the appropriate points covered by the preceding chapters. If the information that the governing body has asked for cannot be produced or is confused, you may draw appropriate conclusions about the quality of leadership and management – unless your request has been unreasonable or unrealistic. The governors who carry out the headteacher's performance management will have another opportunity to judge the effectiveness of his or her leadership. Any doubts you might have may be dispelled or confirmed by the reports from any external adviser you might have bought in during the year.

Improve teaching and learning including the management of pupils' behaviour

Ofsted's Evaluation Schedule states:

> "Inspectors will look for evidence of effective strategies for improving teaching including, where relevant, the teaching of reading and improving behaviour, including:
>
> - seeking out and modelling best practice
> - monitoring the quality of teaching and learning and acting on its findings
> - developing staff through dialogue, coaching, training, mentoring and support
> - leading a coherent programme of professional development
> - leading curriculum development
> - training including, for example, on child protection
> - using appropriate procedures for tackling underperformance."

Improving teaching and learning and the management of pupil behaviour are, or course, operational matters for the staff. However, you will want to know that they are happening (see chapters 3 and 4) and can help school leaders to encourage improvements through the reports you request and the questions you ask, focused on the features that Ofsted has identified as making the most difference in outstanding schools. Teachers learn a lot from observing best practice, discussing what they have seen and how it might apply to their own practice; and even explaining their own best practice. So you should ask for a report which analyses professional development, both already undertaken and planned, to learn how it relates to priorities.

As described in chapter 3 you will want to know that school leaders are monitoring quality, monitoring the effect of their strategies, and, if necessary, identifying further areas for improvement. While you are not entitled to know the names of staff who are under-performing, Ofsted inspectors will almost certainly probe this area.

Improving performance does not just rest on the shoulders of the headteacher and other senior leaders. Middle leaders – subject coordinators in primary schools and heads of department/faculty in secondary schools – should understand their role and be able to describe how they have been helped to develop in that role and what action they have taken to help their colleagues to improve.

Provide a broad and balanced curriculum that meets the needs of all pupils, enables all pupils to achieve their full educational potential and make progress in their learning, and that promotes their good behaviour and safety and their spiritual, moral, social and cultural development

You don't have to be an expert to recognise when the curriculum is not broad and balanced or when it offers little excitement or motivation to pupils. If you are a primary school governor, do you get the impression of a school that is focusing very much on literacy and numeracy; if so, is this a deliberate principle in your curriculum policy? Some schools still believe that this is the way to hold their own in the league tables but there is plenty of evidence that a well-planned, broad and balanced curriculum that really excites children and young people gets the best results. You might start to worry if excitement is squeezed out by SATs preparation in Years 2 and 6.

If you are a secondary school governor, does the Key Stage 3 curriculum build effectively on what pupils have learned at primary school or is there an impression that some pupils are treading water?

You might ask questions such as:

- What opportunities does the school build into the curriculum to help pupils understand enterprise and the world of work? In primary schools there might be a mini-enterprise exercise, with a volunteer coming into school to answer questions about their job. In secondary schools work-related learning is an increasingly important aspect of the curriculum.

- Has the school tried creative approaches to delivery such as using email to send details of homework or using the virtual learning environment to create extra challenge to pupils?

- In Key Stage 4, is there a variety of curriculum pathways to deliver the 14-19 curriculum so that different needs and interests of all students are well catered for? Notwithstanding the pressures on schools to succeed on the more academic EBac measure, there are pupils for whom vocational and work-related learning is more appropriate. Does the school make use of partnerships with other schools, colleges, businesses and agencies to delivery vocational training; and most important, does it really help those students move on to the next stage?

If you are a special school governor your priorities for the students may be quite different from these. In that case it is important for the governing body to review the school's curriculum policy to ensure that all governors share a common understanding with the headteacher and staff of what those priorities are and how far the curriculum is helping to achieve them. Enjoyment and engagement, however, are as important here as anywhere else. You could ask, "Have some or all students been disapplied from any element of the National Curriculum, and is that decision justified by the type and severity of special needs within the school?"

Whatever the phase of your school you might also ask:

- Where do teachers take the opportunity to deliver safety messages in relation to safeguarding, assessing and minimising risk?

- How imaginatively do staff make use of resources, including people and places in the local environment?

- How does a typical student at different stages in the school experience ICT over the course of a week?

- What extra-curricular opportunities for pupils of different ages enrich the curriculum and are there any barriers which prevent some pupils gaining the benefit?

Effective work by the governing body

Although it was not retained in the much slimmer 2012 Inspection Framework, the judgement on governance in the 2009 Framework still provides a useful benchmark for governors to judge themselves:

> "The governing body has the capacity to meet the school's needs and is influential in determining the strategic direction of the school. Governors are rigorous in ensuring that pupils and staff are safe and discharge their statutory duties effectively. They are fully and systematically involved in evaluating the school. Their relationships with staff are constructive and they show determination in challenging and supporting the school in tackling weaknesses and so bringing about necessary improvements. Governors have clear systems for seeking the views of parents and pupils and mechanisms for acting on these."

Reflect on whether the governing body has the capacity to meet the school's needs. Capacity is a product of the skills that individual governors bring to the governing body, the ability of individuals to listen to each other and work as a team, and the commitment to share the work. Effective governors know what questions to ask, are able to listen to and analyse possibly conflicting views, and come to clear collective decisions about the needs of the school and its strategic direction. Capacity building can be developed through training, reading and practice. So, have all governors attended training, including, as a minimum, induction training, and are they all committed to improving their understanding and practice through further training?

The governing body should plan – in partnership with the headteacher – a systematic approach to evaluation which helps to identify priorities for improvement. Do you get the information you need to do your job properly?

Reviewing governing body practice

Looking back on your work over the past two or three years can you find clear evidence that:

- You have taken a strategic view – has your governing body made key decisions and have those decisions really made a difference to your school?
- Your governing body has acted as a critical friend to the school – can you point to instances where you have provided genuine challenge as well as support to the school?
- You have carried out your accountability role – has your governing body held the headteacher and staff to account and have you in your turn provided clear accounts to your parents, pupils, staff and other stakeholders?

Do your minutes clearly indicate that you are carrying out these three roles?

All governing bodies should carry out self-evaluation, preferably annually, so as to identify their own strengths and weaknesses and highlight areas that they should work on. These sessions should also be the opportunity to note and celebrate where the governing body has made a real difference to the school. Many local authorities have developed their own tools for doing this, and there is a standard called GovernorMark that is available to all governing bodies. Accessible at http://glmpartnership.org/governor_mark.html, it provides a useful framework for governing bodies to evaluate their practice and, if they wish, apply for accreditation.

There is nothing in the 2012 Evaluation Schedule that requires inspectors to check that governors have all their statutory policies in place. That does not take away governing bodies' statutory responsibilities but it might help governors to feel less slaves of the checklist. However, inspectors may still want to check that the school is fully compliant, and if there is a particular problem, they might ask to see the relevant policy. So it is still necessary to ensure that your policies are up to date and reflect the school's practice and aspirations.

> **Ofsted's description of outstanding leadership and management**
> The pursuit of excellence in all of the school's activities is demonstrated by an uncompromising and highly successful drive to strongly improve achievement, or maintain the highest levels of achievement, for all pupils including disabled pupils and those who have special educational needs over a sustained period of time. All leaders and managers, including the governing body, are highly ambitious for the school and lead by example. They base their actions on a deep and accurate understanding of the school's performance and of staff and pupils' skills and attributes. Key leaders focus relentlessly on improving teaching and learning, resulting in teaching that is likely to be outstanding and at least consistently good. The school's curriculum provides highly positive, memorable experiences and rich opportunities for high quality learning; has a very positive impact on all pupils' behaviour and safety and contributes very well to pupils' achievement and to their spiritual, moral, social and cultural development. The school has highly successful strategies for engaging with parents and carers, to the very obvious benefit of pupils, including those who might traditionally find working with the school difficult. The school's arrangements for safeguarding pupils meet statutory requirements and give no cause for concern.

Gifted and talented pupils

Around 10 percent of children in every school may be identified as gifted and talented in one way or another and need special challenge and support to reach their full potential. You could ask:

- What is the school's analysis of different gifts and talents of children in each year group?
- What strategies are used with these children and how effective are they?
- Is there anything more the school could be doing and how might the governing body enable this?
- Are parents informed and involved? If not, why not? If so, how much support are they able to give and what views have they expressed?
- What views have been expressed by the pupils themselves?

Special educational needs

Governing bodies have particular statutory responsibilities to ensure that the school provides properly for children with special educational needs, and have to review and report on the effectiveness of their SEN policy each year (though normally the headteacher or SENCO will write this and governors approve). In order to obtain the information about the effectiveness of this provision and to produce this report you might ask the following questions:

- How many children are on School Action, School Action Plus and have SEN statements – and what are the types of special need that the school has to meet?
- How many children have had their SEN status downgraded as a result of successful interventions?
- What does pupil tracking over the past year reveal about the amount of progress made by each pupil with SEN?
- How many hours of teacher assistant time are devoted to supporting specific children's needs?
- How is support provided to achieve maximum inclusion?

- Which agencies help the school to identify and address specific needs and how well does the partnership with those agencies work?
- What training needs have been identified for teachers and TAs and how have they been met?
- What views have been expressed by parents about the progress of children with SEN?
- What views have been expressed by the pupils themselves?
- As a result of this review, what improvements in the policy are highest priority and what action does the school intend to take?

Engage with parents and carers in supporting pupils' achievement, behaviour and safety and their spiritual, moral, social and cultural development

Engagement with parents and carers is clearly a key aspect of leadership and management. There has been a lot of research that shows that parental engagement makes a crucial difference to pupil learning and achievement. If you want parents to work in partnership with the school they need to know what stage their child has reached, what his or her next targets are and how the school can help them to achieve them. Do you know how satisfied your parents are about the quality of the information that they receive on their child's progress? Does the school have systems in place so that information can be exchanged and collaboration develop, such as a home-school diary or text messaging to parents? How effective are the school newsletter and other methods of communication at keeping parents informed and involved?

Schools are not just expected to have two-way communication channels in place but to actively promote their use and to evaluate their effectiveness.

Be prepared to look critically at how the school collects and uses parental views, and to judge how effectively it puts across the message that the school and parents are partners in the children's learning.

Complaints

There is a statutory responsibility for governing bodies to have all relevant complaints and appeals procedures as set out in *A Guide to the Law for School Governors*.

There is a difference between complying with the law and establishing systems that encourage parents and carers to raise genuine concerns. The best customer-focused organisations welcome complaints as a stimulus to continuous improvement, and parental complaints can indicate where policy, practice or communication should be improved. If schools want to demonstrate their belief in parent partnership they will want to respond positively to concerns or complaints wherever possible.

You should expect your school to log concerns and complaints and record how staff have responded so that they can demonstrate how open the school is. Apart from this being good practice, it puts into perspective those rare occasions when the school may respond firmly to unreasonable demands from a difficult parent. You can ask to see an analysis of this data, as well as lists of parental compliments.

Questionnaires

School questionnaires can be targeted on issues that the governing body chooses but can sometimes produce low levels of response. Why don't they work? The table overleaf gives some common reasons.

Problems	Reason	Possible solution
Low response rate	Too many questions	Shorter and more frequent surveys
	Parents don't see the point	Report responses to parents, especially any resulting changes
	Parents busy and/or disorganised	Don't give too much time for response
		Send reminders – text messaging can be very useful
		Ask children to interview parents for homework
		Interview parents at school gate or at parent consultation evenings
We don't hear the views of some parents	Less confidence More disorganised	Interview specific parents or set up a focus group
Some parents don't tell it to us straight	Too much deference	Demonstrate that the school is prepared to change when shortcomings are revealed
	Fear of reprisal	Insist on anonymity

Parent Councils

Some schools have established a Parent Council as a formal consultative body (and in some kinds of trust school they are compulsory). The governing body can set one up, but then must hand over the agenda and leadership to the parents. Parent Councils have the potential to give parents a powerful voice and can assist the parent governors in bringing the parent perspective into the governing body's deliberations. They can also provide a means of explaining the governing body's decisions, policies or actions to parents. For those schools with groups of parents who do not have the confidence to express their views in a larger group, Parent Councils can set up smaller sub-groups. As a governing body you need to consider not only the majority view but opinions of a significant minority if you are to engage all parents and help them to meet their needs, particularly the parents of disadvantaged pupils.

Whether views are collected by questionnaire or through a Parent Council it is vital that parents are informed about the analysis, how it has been considered by the governing body and any decisions taken as a result. Such feedback encourages participation in future consultations.

Ensure that all pupils are safe

What systems does the school have in place for:

- identifying children at risk of significant harm and taking appropriate action
- ensuring safer recruitment, including maintaining the single central record
- following up pupil absence
- maintaining staff awareness and competence to safeguard pupils
- promoting a culture of safety through the curriculum?

Leadership and management

Annual report on safeguarding children

The form may vary over time and between different local authorities but it will ask the following basic information:

Name of Designated Person (senior staff member)

Name of nominated governor

Is the Single Central Record detailing dates of relevant checks on all staff and volunteers working with children up-to-date and accurate?

Summary of training

- to check that all staff have received initial safeguarding training – and refresher training (after two years for designated persons and after three years for all other staff)
- to check that new staff appointed in the past year have all received induction and initial safeguarding training
- to check that staff who appoint new staff and at least one governor have obtained accreditation in Safer Recruitment.

Policies. A checklist of policies is needed to ensure that the school has up-to-date policies relating to safeguarding including:

- anti-bullying
- behaviour management
- drugs and substance misuse
- first aid
- health and safety, including school security
- management of allegations against staff
- PSHE curriculum
- recruitment and selection
- sex education
- staff handbook – guidance on conduct
- use of force and restraint
- whistle-blowing.

Number of referrals made and whether abuse was physical, sexual, emotional or the result of neglect.

Number of children on the Child Protection Register

Number of Looked After Children

Number of allegations made against staff

Finally, there is space to comment on any improvements that need to be made to safeguarding procedures in the school, giving the actions needed and timescales.

If some staff have not received training, for whatever reason, the report must contain a statement about how training gaps will be filled and the timescale.

Governing bodies must evaluate their safeguarding arrangements annually. This is the way to ensure that appropriate arrangements for child protection are in place (see previous page). The report must describe any action that will be taken to tighten up arrangements found to be insecure. Keeping the single central record is an operational matter, but it is important that governors know that it is being kept up to date. Checking the record from scratch is quite complicated but once you are confident that it is correct, it becomes a much more manageable task to check that it reflects any staffing changes made in the intervening months.

As well as damaging a child's education, unauthorised absence can make a child vulnerable and is therefore also a safety issue. You can ask for a report on the procedures for following up absence, especially those for targeting pupils with poor attendance records so that a blip in attendance does not turn into a habit of self-exclusion.

You might ask for an analysis of all the opportunities in curriculum time that teachers and other staff use to introduce and revise the full range of safety messages. At the same time you should check that there is a non-restrictive and bureaucratic safety culture in school, which might include:

- clear procedure for staff to report defects or "near misses" to managers
- procedures for ensuring safety on off-site visits
- procedures to enable the early identification of stress symptoms
- an up-to-date critical incidents policy.

> **Ofsted's description of good leadership and management**
> Key leaders and managers, including the governing body, consistently communicate high expectations and ambition. They model good practice and demonstrably work to monitor, improve and support teaching, encouraging the enthusiasm of staff and channelling their efforts and skills to good effect. As a result, teaching is improving and is at least satisfactory, with much that is good. Planned actions based on accurate self-evaluation to overcome weaknesses have been concerted and effective. As a result, achievement has improved or consolidated previous good performance. The school's curriculum provides well organised, imaginative and effective opportunities for learning for all groups of pupils including disabled pupils and those with special educational needs, promotes positive behaviour and safety and provides a broad range of experiences that contribute well to the pupils' achievement and to their spiritual, moral, social and cultural development. The school usually works well with parents and carers, including those who might traditionally find working with the school difficult, to achieve positive benefits for pupils. The school's arrangements for safeguarding pupils meet statutory requirements and give no cause for concern.

6 Overall effectiveness: the quality of the education provided in the school

Inspectors will make their overall judgement by considering their evaluation of the achievement of pupils (chapter 2), the quality of teaching (chapter 3), the behaviour and safety of pupils (chapter 4), the quality of leadership and management of the school (chapters 2–5) and the extent to which the school meets the needs of range of pupils at the school.

You should also be aware that, in the words of the 2012 Evaluation Schedule, the school's overall effectiveness will be judged on "how well the school promotes all pupils' spiritual, moral, social and cultural development by providing positive experiences through planned and coherent opportunities in the curriculum and through interactions with teachers and other adults" to:

- "reflect on the experiences provided by the school, use their imagination and creativity, and develop curiosity in their learning
- develop and apply an understanding of right and wrong in their school life and life outside school
- take part in a range of activities requiring social skills
- gain a well-informed understanding of the options and challenges facing them as they move through the school and on to the next stage of their education and training
- overcome barriers to their learning
- respond positively to a range of artistic, sporting and other cultural opportunities, provided by the school including, for example, developing an appreciation of theatre, music and literature
- develop the skills and attitudes to enable them to participate fully and positively in democratic, modern Britain
- understand and appreciate the range of different cultures within school and further afield as an essential element of their preparation for life."

> **Below the bottom line – Ofsted's description of inadequate**
> Overall effectiveness is likely to be inadequate if any of the following apply.
> - Achievement is inadequate.
> - Quality of teaching is inadequate.
> - Behaviour and safety are inadequate.
> - Leadership and management are inadequate.
> - There are important weaknesses in the school's promotion of pupils' spiritual, moral, social and cultural development, resulting in a poor climate for learning and an incohesive school community where pupils or groups of pupils are unable to thrive.

Governing bodies can help the staff to collect evidence to demonstrate that pupils **reflect on the experiences provided by the school, use their imagination and creativity, and develop curiosity in their learning**. Visiting governors can do what inspectors will increasingly do, which is talk with a group of pupils after a lesson, asking them to show the work they have done in that lesson and explain what they have learned. For example, in looking at creativity governors could seek evidence from talking to pupils and staff to enable them to answer:

- How important is music in our school curriculum? What is the range and quality of artwork?
- Does it show individual pupil creativity as well as developing technique?
- Do young people have good opportunity to develop skills in dance and drama?
- Are pupils encouraged to find creative and enterprising solutions to problems in a range of subjects?

After the events in August 2011, Britain asked itself, how could so many young people and adults become opportunistic looters? Governors should ask how effective their school is in helping pupils to **develop and apply an understanding of right and wrong in their school life and life outside school**. And they may be able to collect evidence by observing (or hearing reports about):

- pupils as they debate moral dilemmas – the governing body might establish a (team) prize for a project which addresses a dilemma
- discussion and actions on issues such as recycling and energy conservation
- responsible behaviour including evidence of young people looking after each other
- debate on issues such as global inequalities and sustainability.

A report from the Institute for Public Policy Research, *Freedom's Orphans* (2006), pointed out that even if students gain good qualifications they may have unequal life chances because of a lack of "soft skills". You can ask for the school to analyse **the range of activities requiring social skills**, to evaluate their impact and to consider whether there is scope to develop them further.

Another obstacle to some pupils succeeding as well as their peers in other schools is the variable quality of advice from teachers and other adults about the **options and challenges facing them as they move through the school and on to the next stage of their education and training**. There are examples of schools where expectations of exciting futures are dangled before pupils as they start secondary school – or even before – and the routes to achieving ambitious aims are set out for them. Governors will want to satisfy themselves that curriculum pathways at Year 10 and

---

Ofsted's description of outstanding school effectiveness

The school's practice consistently reflects the highest aspirations for pupils and expectations of staff. It ensures that best practice is spread effectively in a drive for continuous improvement. Teaching is likely to be outstanding and together with a rich curriculum, which is highly relevant to pupils' needs, it contributes to outstanding learning and achievement or, in exceptional circumstances, achievement that is good and rapidly improving. Other principal aspects of the school's work are good or outstanding. The school's thoughtful and wide ranging promotion of the pupils' spiritual, moral, social and cultural development enables them to thrive in a supportive, highly cohesive learning community. Consequently, pupils and groups of pupils have excellent experiences at school, ensuring that they are very well equipped for the next stage of their education, training or employment.

Year 12 and the advice pupils receive allow them to fulfil their potential. You may invite an outsider, consultant or senior staff member from another school to provide an independent report.

Soft skills such as perseverance, problem-solving and ability to take advice and learn from mistakes are important to enable young people to **overcome barriers to their learning**. You can ask for a brief report on the ways that the school develops those skills, particularly with pupils who find learning most difficult. The governing body would probably enjoy hearing about success stories and strategies that worked particularly well. It will also benefit staff who prepare those reports to remember their successes and reflect on the lessons that could be applied to other students.

All pupils have an entitlement to a rich experience during the school day and afterwards, and it is some of the young people who would benefit most who miss out – whether because the school does not offer a rich diet or because those pupils think the after-school offer is not for them. You should ensure that there is **a range of artistic, sporting and other cultural opportunities provided by the school** and that these are being taken up by the pupils. You might ask:

- How many children are learning to play an instrument? What range of instruments is available? How many sing in choirs (the human voice is a free musical instrument)?
- How are pupils introduced to theatre through visiting drama groups and going to theatres?
- How much use does the school make of visiting artists and speakers and how many visits do pupils make to art galleries and museums?
- What are the opportunities for practising sport, including competitions?

Governors may use direct observation by attending some of these artistic, sporting and cultural events and discussing their experience with pupils. Since obtaining sufficient adult supervision is sometimes an impediment to these activities, the attendance of one or more governors may be of practical use as well. Another impediment may be funding and the inability of children entitled to free school meals to make a sufficient contribution to the cost. This might be an appropriate use of pupil premium funds.

It is important that schools start to prepare young people and **develop the skills and attitudes to enable them to participate fully and positively in democratic, modern Britain**. Governors may ask for a report on any work they are doing to help pupils understand citizenship. Is there good evidence of pupils' interest in a democratic process – where interest in the activity of the School Council and other pupil consultative activity is not confined to a small group? How representative of the school population are the School Council members? What issues does the School Council deal with and how much are those issues identified by the young people themselves? How well thought-out are the decisions or recommendations? What changes in the school can be tracked back to pupil views?

Evidence can be found in School Council minutes, from inviting School Council members to meet with governors or by governors seeking an invitation to attend School Council meetings themselves. There are often conclusions to be drawn from direct observation.

Pupils need to **understand and appreciate the range of different cultures within school and further afield as an essential element of their preparation for life**. The curriculum will include examples of diversity but you should ask to see evidence of their impact. These may include governors:

- observing the engagement of different groups with each other outside the classroom
- taking part with pupils in events which bring them into contact with groups not

represented in the immediate community and discussing the experience with pupils

- hearing young people talk about what they have learned from contacts with people from communities different from their own – in the UK and abroad.

Another way to establish overall effectiveness is to look at the progression and destination of pupils when they leave school. This is the proof of the pudding: showing the cumulative impact of all those high expectations as pupils move through primary and secondary education, the success of the school in overcoming any barriers to learning, the advice and support schools give to help young people plot their course and develop the soft skills which enable them to get there. It's worth taking time to analyse and discuss the destination data the headteacher supplies. Celebrate the successes where leavers have gone on to further education or where leavers have secured apprenticeships or jobs with training; consider what can be done to prevent further leavers falling into the "Not in Employment, Education or Training" (NEET) category. What more could the school have done to meet the needs of those young people, and what lessons are there for the education of similar students still at school?

Governors who take such analysis seriously will want to take a long-term view of destinations, tracking former students who have moved to FE college and, if possible looking at the prospects/fortunes of the young people who secured jobs or were seeking employment when they left school.

Ofsted's description of good school effectiveness

The school takes effective action to enable most pupils to reach their potential. Pupils benefit from teaching that is at least good. This promotes very positive attitudes to learning and ensures that achievement is at least good. Leadership and management play a significant role in this and are good overall. Behaviour and safety are strong features. Deliberate and effective action is taken to create a cohesive learning community by promoting the pupils' spiritual, moral, social and cultural development. A positive climate for learning exists and pupils and groups of pupils have highly positive experiences at school so that they are well prepared for the next stage in their education, training or employment.

7 Turning self-evaluation into school improvement

Planning for school improvement has often been made to look a complex process, which has made it difficult for many governing bodies to engage in a proper strategic involvement. For governors, the aim should be to keep it simple.

In many ways we have already done the hard part. Asking for and collecting the evidence, as described in this book, provides a shared understanding of what the school does well and what it needs to do to improve. The Ofsted Framework and Evaluation Schedule also help to make it easy by focusing on a very few key factors that inspectors have learned make the biggest impact on pupil outcomes: namely the quality of teaching, pupil behaviour and attendance, and a relentless focus on both by leaders and managers. Some other conditions underpin these, including pupils feeling secure and the curriculum being appropriate, but once those have been put in place, schools will make the improvements they seek by focusing on teaching, behaviour and attendance – and the greatest of these is teaching.

Of course, there are lots of elements to good teaching, as described in chapter 3, and it is the quality of your school self-evaluation that will help you to see which levers to pull for school improvement. Looking at pupil outcomes, as described in chapter 2, may give you some clues about the areas where the school's practice is most in need of improvement.

As you work your way through school self-evaluation, you will have been able to tick off aspects where the school has already collected good evidence and your collective knowledge is secure. There will be other aspects that you will have prioritised for further evaluation. But the school cannot afford to wait for you to get the full picture, nor should you. On the basis of the evaluation that you are able to make now, you should be able to identify something that you know needs to be worked on urgently; and that should go into your plan.

The sample Summary School Improvement Planner overleaf provides a format that gives senior leaders a common understanding, at a glance, of the agreed areas for improvement, the aspects of the school that have been prioritised for further or deeper evaluation, and the information that the governing body expects to see relating to those. Behind this summary, there will be more detailed plans specifying the area for improvement, the actions that the school will take, the timescales, resources (including time) that will be made available, the success criteria, and the monitoring and evaluation arrangements. All that detail is essentially a management tool. Governors may look at this detail before approving the plan, to check that the success criteria are clear and that timescales and resourcing are realistic, but it is essentially operational; what governors should focus on is the summary.

Sample School Improvement Plan Summary

School vision:

date:

Our current judgement	Priorities for improvement	Focus for further evaluation	Information to the GB	What?	When?
Our analysis of pupil outcomes leads us to judge pupil achievement as …		The priority for deeper and more detailed evaluation in the coming year is …			
Currently based on pupil outcomes we believe teaching is … We believe we have sufficient evidence to say that …	We have sufficient evidence to identify that an area for improvement is …	We will collect further evidence over this coming year to obtain a better understanding of …			
Our evaluation of behaviour is that it is generally …	but it could be improved in the following respects:	Our priority for more detailed evaluation in the coming year relates to …			
Our evaluation of leadership and management is that it is … We believe we have sufficient evidence relating to the following aspects of L&M:	Our evaluation suggests that a priority for this year is to …	Our priority for more detailed evaluation in the coming year relates to the following areas:			

8 Getting the most from Ofsted inspection

A governing body that has been working in partnership with the headteacher and senior leaders on robust self-evaluation and has agreed plans to improve key areas will have enabled its school to take Ofsted inspection in its stride.

Taking into account the views of parents, staff and pupils

In the current inspection regime inspectors will give greater consideration to the views of parents, pupils and staff as important evidence.

The parents' questionnaire now has: 12 statements inviting parents to indicate strongly agree, agree, disagree or strongly disagree; a thirteenth question on whether the parent would recommend the school to another parent – Yes, No; and a final section for parents to enlarge on any questions they choose. The statements marked by an asterisk are new to the 2012 questionnaire.

1. My child feels safe at this school.
2. My child is making good progress at this school.
3. This school meets my child's particular needs.
4. This school ensures my child is well looked after.*
5. My child is taught well at this school.*
6. This school helps my child to develop skills in communication, reading, writing and mathematics.*
7. There is a good standard of behaviour at this school.
8. My child's lessons are not disrupted by bad behaviour.*
9. This school deals with any cases of bullying effectively. (Bullying includes persistent name-calling, cyber, racist and homophobic bullying.)*
10. This school helps me to support my child's learning.
11. This school responds well to my concerns.
12. This school keeps me well informed.

In October 2011 Ofsted launched Parent View, an on-line survey that covers the same areas. It enables parents to express views about their child's school at any time between inspections. Any pattern that emerges from either the survey or parent questionnaire will indicate lines of enquiry to be followed during an inspection. With no-notice inspections this on-line survey will be even more important as many of the questionnaires issued to parents at the start of the inspection are likely to be returned after the inspectors have departed. You should encourage all parents to complete the on-line survey so that it is representative of parents' views, and governing bodies should study the results to identify any issues that require further attention.

Similarly, the even greater attention that Ofsted requires its inspectors to pay to pupil views should make you more determined than ever to give pupils a voice and listen to their concerns.

The sorts of questions that staff are asked by inspectors reveals information that the governing body would be advised to ascertain and respond to:

1. I am proud to be a member of staff at this school.
2. My contribution to the school is valued.
3. I know what we are trying to achieve as a school.
4. I am involved in what the school is trying to achieve.
5. I contribute to the school's process of self-evaluation.
6. The school makes appropriate provision for my professional development.
7. The school is well led.
8. Governors do an effective job in this school.
9. The school runs smoothly on a daily basis.
10. Children are safe in this school.
11. Any unacceptable behaviour by pupils is consistently well managed.
12. The school successfully meets the differing needs of individual pupils.

The above questions were used in 2011. In the light of the changed focus you may wish to check staff views on how frequently lessons are disrupted by poor behaviour and how well the school deals with all types of bullying.

No judgements are made on the basis of questionnaire evidence alone. The information gained may lead to lines of enquiry, and if a significant proportion of responses have indicated a problem, inspectors will report whether, on the basis of other evidence, they agree or disagree.

Being "inspection ready"

Inspectors aim, as far as possible, to see the school at work normally. All schools receive a maximum of two working days' notice, but it is likely that all inspections will be "no notice" from September 2012. The lead inspector will want to speak with the headteacher or, if the head is away for any reason, the deputy or teacher in charge of the school for that day about the practicalities of conducting the inspection, and will ask to see key documents which demonstrate school self-evaluation and improvement plans.

Governing bodies can help the senior leadership team and staff to prepare for the inspection and can ensure that governors yourselves are ready.

First, if the school has not organised its self-evaluation into an up-to-date and accessible record that can be emailed (or, in the case of no-notice inspection, handed) to the lead inspector, the inspection will kick off with a lot of stress for the headteacher, and the lack will suggest that the school leadership, including governing body, does not have a clear idea of how the school can be improved. You should help to avoid this difficulty by ensuring that the reports you have requested and other evidence collected are well organised. If your headteacher operates in a "creative muddle", a governor with a particular interest or skill might help the head with this; or it may be a project for a member of the administration staff released from their other duties with some temporary cover.

Secondly, there is no time for the school to be spruced up and wall displays refreshed. The problem with giving even a few days' notice is that in many schools the staff worked flat out and came in over the weekend to smarten the school up. Inspectors want to see what the pupils experience on a daily basis. If the school is normally untidy with old and tattered displays, inspectors need to know. You can help here by asking whether there is a clear rationale for display and procedures for ensuring that they are regularly changed, and whether there is a de-cluttering policy. The headteacher could commission one or more governors to make an unannounced visit and report to the head on their impressions of tidiness and display. You will not be doing this for Ofsted – but because it will make for a better environment in which children and adults can work and learn all the time.

Next, the headteacher may be out of school, on a course, say, or off sick. Is the proper professional understanding of the school held exclusively by a single leader or is it shared across the staff? Do senior members of staff have the commitment and capacity to welcome the inspection team? If not, as a governing body you need to help the head to develop them and to put contingency plans in place. You might work with the headteacher on a plan to give a senior member of staff practice in explaining the school. This might include making a presentation to governors on some key elements of the school self-evaluation with the headteacher taking a back seat to observe and encourage.

Fourthly, there may be no time to find an appropriate space for the inspectors to use as their base and to provide facilities such as coffee- and tea-making. Even in inspections with some days' notice this can be a real headache, especially for very small schools. Giving up the headteacher's office may seem to be the easiest solution but if it then means that he or she cannot operate normally it rather defeats the object and, even worse, may make it more difficult for the headteacher to find additional information that inspectors may request. Is there a small meeting room that could be used and where the activities normally taking place in that room could be relocated?

Next, in some schools, parking is a serious difficulty; thinking about how to solve the problem in advance can get the inspection off to a smooth start. The governing body can help the school by asking what contingency plans are in place if inspectors were to arrive tomorrow. Does everyone know the plan and understand their role in making it work?

Finally, you need to be ready to meet inspectors. The governing body should organise a communication tree so that all governors can be informed that an inspection is imminent or has already started, and should agree a list of governors showing the order in which they should be contacted. This should mean that at least one of them can make themselves available to talk with inspectors and attend the feedback at the end of the second day. It may be sensible for the chair of governors to be in mobile phone contact. There needs to be somebody in the office primed to implement the procedure as soon as it is known that inspectors are coming.

Governor attendance at the feedback meeting

Feedback at the end of the inspection is a valuable opportunity for you to hear what inspectors intend to write in their report. At least one governor should attend and inspectors should welcome more than one as an indication of governor engagement. In fact, the engagement of the headteacher throughout the inspection process means that there will be little new for him or her to learn, and it is governors who will learn most from the feedback.

The feedback provides an excellent opportunity for governors to seek clarification. The better governors understand what inspectors mean by the statements in their now very brief reports, the more will it help them to understand their school, either to confirm that their view has been correct all along or to indicate that the school has been too modest or has over-rated itself in one or more categories.

> **The timing of inspections**
>
> In order to concentrate inspection on those schools in most need of improvement, some satisfactory schools will be inspected ahead of the three year norm, good schools which maintain standards may have the inspection interval extended, while the 2011 Education Act allows outstanding schools to be exempt.
>
> *How soon after your last inspection are inspectors likely to return?*
>
> | Previous Ofsted judgement | Return likely after: | Notes |
> |---|---|---|
> | Special measures | First monitoring visit after 4-6 months; re-inspection after 24-28 months | Will be earlier if inspection revealed safeguarding issue |
> | Notice to improve | Monitoring visit after 6-8 months | Re-inspection after 12-16 months |
> | Satisfactory | Monitoring inspection between 12 and 24 months | For a "significant proportion of schools judged satisfactory" |
> | | Full inspection within three school years | All schools judged satisfactory |
> | Good | Within five school years | Unless Ofsted deems it should be inspected earlier |
> | Good special school or PRU | Within three school years | Also applies to schools which cater for pupils 0–3 years. |
> | Outstanding | Exempt from Section 5 inspection | Unless HMCI deems it should be inspected under Section 8 of the Education Act 2005, or teaching as only deemed "good" |
>
> *Under proposals at the time of publication, the "satisfactory" and "notice to improve" categories will be abolished in September 2012 and be replaced by "requires improvement", and schools in this category will be re-inspected in 12–15 months.*
>
> *For the criteria for Ofsted to bring forward the inspection of a good or outstanding school, see the Ofsted website, www.ofsted.gov.uk*

Conclusion

As a governor you give up your time voluntarily, whether on cold, rainy nights or balmy summer evenings, because you share with headteachers and staff a deep desire to help get the best for children and young people. Ofsted inspection is the public validation of the efforts of senior leaders, including governors and staff, working in partnership with parents to achieve those ends. The report enables governors to celebrate and encourage all that is good, and helps them to rectify and improve those aspects of the school which prevent pupil outcomes being as good or as outstanding as they can be.

Previous inspection frameworks have helped to educate headteachers and governors and raise expectations. Each time the bar has been raised. This should be welcome if it helps us to improve outcomes for all pupils. It is a challenge worth rising to. It is hoped that this book has provided sufficient practical advice to help the pro-active and strategic among you to play your part in that improvement.

Appendixes

A Inspection of faith schools

Schools which are designated as having a religious character have religious aspects inspected separately under Section 48 of the 2005 Education Act. In Anglican and Methodist schools the inspection is referred to as a SIAS inspection (School Inspection in Anglican Schools). Although legally Section 48 inspections only cover RE and worship, the inspections are widened in Catholic schools to cover all aspects of the Catholic life of the school. Schools designated as having a religious character now include Jewish, Hindu, Muslim, Seventh-day Adventist and Sikh schools.

Heads or chairs of governors are expected to inform their diocesan or other appropriate schools service as soon as they know they will be inspected by Ofsted and it is up to the school to then commission a SIAS or Section 48 inspection. Dioceses maintain a pool of approved and trained inspectors and provide information packs setting out contractual conditions. In earlier rounds of school inspections the religious aspect was often carried out concurrently, but as the period of notice has shrunk this has become less feasible and so it is more likely to be in the following term.

Schools can claim a grant from the DfE to cover the cost of inspection of RE and worship. Catholic schools have to find the additional cost of inspecting the Catholic life of the school.

B Inspection of boarding provision

The boarding aspects of school with residential provision are inspected under the Framework for Inspecting Boarding and Residential Provision in schools, 2011. This covers

- Overall effectiveness
- Outcomes for boarders
- Quality of boarding provision and care
- Boarders' safety
- Leadership and management of boarding.

These inspections are in addition to normal inspection.

Index

absence 44
academies 9
accountability 7, 39
artistic opportunities 47
assessment 26–7
attainment 15, 18–20
attendance 33–4

baseline testing 12
basic characteristics of a school 11–12
behaviour 7, 29–34, 37
boarding schools 55
broad and balanced curriculum 35, 38–41
bullying 7, 30–31

capability 28
child protection 37, 44, 52
community 48
complaints 41
creativity 46
curriculum 10, 23, 26, 35, 37, 38–41, 44, 45, 46, 49

disability 23, 29, 31–2, 33
diversity 47

Early Years Foundation Stage 27
Early Years Foundation Stage Profile 12
English as an additional language 23
Equality Act 2010 31
Evaluation Schedule 8, 21, 22, 36, 39, 49
exclusions 31

faith schools 55
feedback meeting 53–4
Fischer Family Trust 11, 16-18
floor standards 20
free school meals 11, 14, 23, 33

gangs 32
gender 16, 30
gifted and talented pupils 40
governor visits 27

"hard to reach" groups 36
homework 24

inspection 49–52
Inspection Framework 29, 39, 49

knives 32

leadership 35–44
league tables 38
local authorities 38
looked after children 33, 42

management 35–44
middle leaders 37
monitoring 11

National College 27
National Curriculum 10–11
NEET 48
no-notice inspections 52

Ofsted Annual Report 22, 25–6
Ofsted descriptors 8–9
overall effectiveness 45–8

P scales 21
Parent Councils 42
Parent View 51
parent/carer support 36
parents' questionnaire 41–2, 51
policies 36, 42, 43
punctuality 33–4
pupil attainment 7
Pupil progress 11–12, 14–16
pupil questionnaires 31
pupil survey 26
pupil tracking 11

questionnaires 31, 41–2, 51, 52

RAISEonline 11–15, 33
reading standards 19
risk management 32–3

safeguarding 42–4
safety of pupils 29–34
SATs 23
School Council 30–31, 36, 47
School Governance: Learning from the best 6
school improvement 49–50
school improvement plan 9, 14, 49, 50
SEF 5
self-evaluation 5–9
SEN register 14
special educational needs 20–21, 24, 31–2, 33, 40–41
special schools 21, 38
spiritual, moral, social and cultural development 41, 46
sporting opportunities 47
staff questionnaire 52
stakeholders 5
subject coordinators 37
substance misuse 32
support staff 23–4, 30

teaching quality 22–8
timing of inspections 52
tracking pupil progress 15–16
traffic lights 16

value added 12-13
views of parents 11, 31, 39, 41-2, 51
views of pupils 11, 36, 39, 40–41, 47, 51

weaknesses 5, 7, 8, 25, 39, 45
"whiskers" 13